EARTH UP YOUR
Roots

poeMS, short stories & a play

Selin Senol Akin

SELIN SENOL-AKIN

Copyright ©2022 SELIN SENOL-AKIN

All Rights Reserved

No part of this book may be reproduced, or stored in a retrieval system, or transmitted in any form or by any means, electronic, mechanical, photocopying, recording, or otherwise, without express written permission of the publisher, except in the case of brief quotations embodied in critical reviews and certain other noncommercial uses permitted by copyright law.

ISBN: 9781734656343

Author Photography by: Engin Tufan Sevimli

Cover illustration: Mert Bil
Inside illustration: Dalya Akin

PRINTED IN THE UNITED STATES OF AMERICA

EARTH UP YOUR ROOTS

to my 'dahlia' flower Dalya…

planted in a conventional union,
blooming under unconventional watering

SELIN SENOL-AKIN

to earth up your roots
  rather than deem them a 'lost cause'
    can bud the sweetest botany

FOREWORD

Dear fellow seedling of the earth we inhabit,

Do your roots anchor you so tightly you cannot flow free in the wind? Or, do they ground you steadily, yet loosely enough to allow swaying toward your own way, instead…?

A plant, if ripped with its roots intact- can be replanted: allowed to flourish elsewhere… Unlike one cut off from its roots completely. Sometimes we must accept and carry along the 'rotting' (or even already 'rotten') portions of the seeds that have formed us through our lineages and early environments.

No culture or family is without flaws- no matter how they may manage to make it appear on the surface. Yet it is with our flaws that we are unique and able to experience life through a unique perspective- ultimately making us more intriguing and fulfilled.

Denial is painful, while acceptance is freedom. We can relocate our 'roots' if we must- in order to possibly avoid toxicity or stagnation, and flourish- but must keep them nonetheless, in order to bloom. And mine?

SELIN SENOL-AKIN

my roots are Mustafa Kemal [1]
my roots are the Balkans
my roots are the Huns, the Hittites…
as well as the Byzantines and Ottomans

my roots are tragedy,
both victory
and controversy

my roots include both the fungi
and the nutrients-
some better to bury
others, shared, like a berry

the good and the wrong
the silenced and the song
before a microphone

my roots are mistakes
raised stakes
heartbreaks
yet doing whatever it takes

undeniable
uncrushable

---

[1] Atatürk: founder of the modern Turkish republic

In this, my third poetic compilation, I present you, dear reader, with various symbolic short stories from my subconscious, adding to the purely poetic-verse setup of *Write Out Your Drops*, and the memoir alongside the poetry of *Set Free Your Flow*.

'The Rose Moon', for example, presents a forbidden romance between an Armenian boy, Tigran, and a Turkish girl, Gülay- in the backdrop of both the tragic events of 1915 as well as the historically-subsequent expulsion of Turkish Muslims from Bulgaria. This was one of the first stories I had written, having intended to develop the love story into a novel- until 'The Catalyst' storyline took over my mind during my time spent in Norway.

I've comprised the first three sections of this compilation through interweaving two short stories in each one with 'root'-themed poetry. The 4th section, *Upkeep*, has a longer story, 'Ordinary', which was first published in a multiple-author anthology named 'Flash' in 2020 (I'd written it during the Fall of 2019 right before the pandemic) and later in the 'Journal of Academics & Fiction' for New York's *The Media High School* in 2021.

Finally…there's 'Zelle' of the last section: my sole play. Just as the intrigue of Mata Hari herself- the controversial historical figure at once political and representative of dance-holds a special meaning for me, so does this piece as my first attempt at a short play. Few know I was an aspiring actress as a college student and later in my early 20's. I participated in theatrical performances and took various acting classes- including a summer program at the New York Film Academy. But, as so often occurs, *life is said to be what happens when you're busy making other plans*, and I'm so much happier and more creatively-fulfilled writing now.

Yet I'd love for someone to play out my stories one day. Life is also said to *imitate art…* as well as at times to *be stranger than fiction*.

> *what's out of control, can control you*
> *what you can't love, can leave you*
> *what your eyes won't see, can seize you*
> *if you don't live life, life can outlive you*

Here's hoping these words will 'root' themselves in your soul after you've read them, and inspire you to 'bloom' your own flowers- all the while as you ***Earth Up[2] Your Roots.***

---

[2] *earth up*- to gather soil around the base of a plant in order to promote protection and growth.

EARTH UP YOUR ROOTS

we can't expect roots to ground us,
magnificent birds to surround us

or flowers to bloom from our deeds
without first planting the seeds

XOXO,

Selin Senol-Akin

SELIN SENOL-AKIN

TABLE OF CONTENTS

1: PLANT 11-30

2: BUD 31-66

3: REAP 67-104

4: UPKEEP 105-134

5: BLOOM 135-166

EARTH UP YOUR ROOTS

PLANT

*and sometimes you can feel
like a little puppy
groomed yet doomed
begging in the shop window
for the smiling passerby to adopt you*

SELIN SENOL-AKIN

branches-
leafed, visible, mighty
extended creators and majestic figures
on the earth, endurant- with shadows
nifty enough to shade those wishing to inhabit
the green-brown
embrace
for brief
solitude
and contemplation,
the limbs
of nature
mirroring
themselves
across the porous soil-
branching out as a root system
underneath the earth that is
unleafed, invisible, yet even mightier

*Inspired by 'The Oak Tree' by Johnny Ray Ryder Jr

EARTH UP YOUR ROOTS

multiple elements exist
for the hatchling to avoid leaving the nest

                                        it flies anyway

multiple dawns signify the end
of the most beautiful nights

                            the sun shines anyway

you, grounded, stay
while they, undecided, stray

despite lingering pain
more loss palpable than gain-

                            you blossom each day

SELIN SENOL-AKIN

THE ANT

LATE SUMMER, 2005

"...FOUR...FIVE...SIX! OOH, I BEAT YOU!" Skipping stones across the waves was one of the past times Ömer had missed the most from his childhood home by the Aegean Sea.

He felt grateful that his new buddy in London, Mark, was there with him once again on that cloudy day in September by the River Thames.

"Only because I let you win!" Mark snickered, interrupting Ömer's indulged reverie. His eyes caught something moving farther ahead. "Mate, look at that big ant on the rock over there! Who's going to squish it first?"

"Mark! Did you know that if you kill even a tiny little ant, you will pay the price for it?" Ömer shook his head as he looked at the direction where Mark had been pointing, seeing the tiny doomed animal flurrying about.

"What?" Mark smirked, fiddling with a smooth pebble. "Oh, please. How many ants have all of us likely killed on a daily basis- without knowing- just walking down the street?"

"And how do you know you haven't paid for it?" Ömer raised his eyebrow.

"What do you mean?"

"Well, let's say everything was going just fine one day, for example, right?" Ömer's eyes were lit up as he responded. "And suddenly you tripped while walking- how do you know that wasn't your punishment?" He flashed an all-knowing smile.

"Punishment?" Mark's mouth was now hanging open.

"My uncle- Mehmet *amca*- told me that life is a test, did you know that?" Ömer's tossed a random pebble out toward the water. He's back in Izmir. I miss him. He always says: *if we do good, we get rewarded, and if we do bad, we get punished.* Right here on this earth, he says-even before death and before heaven or hell. That life is like a video game. I mean, you never think about this stuff?"

"I don't know, mate," Mark squirmed his face. "We're twelve, not twenty, or…old- like forty or something!"

"My *amca* says 40 is not old…"

"*Aja*?" Mark snickered. "Oh, you mean your uncle? Sorry, mate, you know I suck with Turkish words you share with me. Well, he must be old to say such a thing! Huh!"

"It's pronounced *am- ja*" Ömer enunciated, rolling his eyes. "And my uncle is not old at all. Plus, he knows things. He reads a lot."

"Oh, yeah?" Mark crossed his arms. "Well, my mom tells me 'dem religious folks peach what they don't do!"

"You mean…*preach*?" Ömer began to laugh so hard he had to hold his jiggling stomach.

"What's so funny?" Mark's face had finally turned serious.

"Nothing mate, sorry," Ömer cleared his throat. "Look…all I know is- from this day on- because now you *know* and can no longer be excused by the ignorance of sin- your punishment will likely be twofold. Now that you *know* you cannot kill even an insect- unless you sense an immediate danger to you and you do so purely in self-defense- you will pay some level of price for it if you do…"

"Ignorance of sin? Okay, mate…" Mark scratched behind his ear. He got up to his feet. "The sun is going down. My mom's expecting me home for dinner."

"It isn't even 16:00, Markie," Ömer checked his watch, puzzled. "The sun won't set until…"

"We eat early…" Mark interrupted.

"Well, um, alright…" Ömer took in a deep breath. "See you at soccer practice tomorrow?"

Ömer watched as Mark threw in a quick smile behind him with a wave as his body sped toward the block of his apartment.

He'd never see the face of his friend again for another ten years.

§

SELIN SENOL-AKIN

LATE SUMMER, 2015

"Turn the volume up, Zehra," Ömer insisted. His wife was still busy talking on the phone with her mother in Bursa, not allowing for him to hear the BBC news very well. He placed his palm on his forehead and shook his head.

Ömer could envision the two of them as an older couple already- and, unfortunately, it wasn't looking too promising. Beauty, morals, kindness- not to mention great cooking- Ömer loved many of the traits Zehra possessed. Of that, he was sure. But in regards to whether or not she'd actually been his intellectual equal was up for debate, as far as he was concerned.

"Zehra!" Ömer raised his voice with a sterner look in her direction this time, extending his bare feet onto the glass table in the center of the sofas. He exhaled with a satisfied glee, allowing his head to fall back onto the sofa cushion.

Zehra's wooden slippers clicked and clacked their way closer to him. "Momma says hello too, by the way!" she nudged, plopping down adjacent to her husband. She handed Ömer the remote control she'd brought with her from across the room.

"I just talked to *Fatma anne* yesterday!" Ömer protested, scratching his head. "I'm tired!" He added a smile before Zehra could protest.

"Okay, my lazy love," Zehra rolled her eyes, returning his smile with a wink. "Let's watch the news."

Scrolling down a plethora of talent shows and soap operas listed on the Guide, Ömer had decided on the local news channel. Besides, he knew it'd soon be ending, to be followed by his favorite cop show. He reached his arms across Zehra as the two shared a chuckle over the image of a child making a funny face while hugging a puppy- part of a final commercial before the familiar news anchor continued with a stern face.

"*Yok artık….!*" Ömer got up with a jolt as a photograph of a familiar face flashed across the scene.

"*Aşkım*? What's the matter?"

"The body of Mark Kensington, just 22 years old, was discovered yesterday morning at the construction site," the woman with a well-coiffed blonde bob was saying. "His mother had difficulty identifying him, as his face was gnawed nearly unrecognizable by carpenter ants."

"Ants?" Zehra was shaking her head, turning to lock eyes with her husband. She couldn't, as Ömer's peepers were frozen on the screen. "Who's that? What's going on?"

"That's him," Ömer was mumbling. "I follow him on Facebook."

"The police are still investigating the nature of the case, as it is not clear whether the further damage to the face occurred after his death or not," the presenter continued. "The exact cause of this horrific death is still uncertain at the moment. Authorities are asking anyone with any information to call…"

- - - - - - - -

THE TREE WOMAN

SPRING, 1912

THE WOMAN'S FRAIL HANDS caressed the callused, strong ones of her fiancée's. "I will always be with you, my beloved." Celeste Frost's amber eyes teared at the sight of Robert Carlisle's strong jawline and baby blues. "I will caress your cheeks with the blowing breeze, keep you warm through rays of the sun directly hitting your arms, tickle your face through a drop of rain when you're feeling dry and parched…."

"Do not speak of these things, my canary," the handsome carpenter before her replied softly. Celeste loved it when Robert would call her that. He knew she adored singing.

"We *will* get married this summer as planned," Robert went on. "You *will* become a beautiful bride, and soon after- a wonderful mother. The mother of a little child who will get to see her survive and be strong for our family. I need you. We will need you. The female bird makes a home."

"And all birds need a nest, Robert," Celeste spoke softly, gazing at the body of water in the near distance. She leaned her body onto the nearest bark. "They need the trees. I think I shall be a part of this tree most of all, Robert. Overlooking New Rochelle Harbor where we both grew up. Providing shade and shelter when you feel unsafe…Promise me, Robert, to never cut it down."

"Rest assured, my darling," Robert tucked a strand of Celeste's raven locks behind her ear. "In the unlikely event that this wicked cancer does beat us, I shall never betray your wishes."

"I wrote a poem, Robert, do you want to hear it?" Celeste forced herself to smile, licking quickly the teardrop that had befallen her cheek.

"Hush, my darling," Robert placed a gentle finger on her blush-pink, pale-leaning lips. "We've conversed long enough. You must save

EARTH UP YOUR ROOTS

your breath. Your precious lungs...Perhaps we should go inside our chambers and..."

"Robert, please..." Celeste insisted, adding a playful pout. Upon his encouraging smile in return, she started to recite her poem:

> *oh, to be like a tree...*
> *rooted,*
> *yet with branches allowed to sway*
> *shedding old leaves*
> *with multiple chances*
> *to begin a new*
> *and lean a new way*

"That was beautiful, sweetheart," Robert squeezed her cheek with affection. "If not my canary singing around it: then at least you shall be my rooted tree for evermore. Around for many years. You'll see."

§

SPRING, 1913

"Ow!" Lenore exclaimed, looking up as

she brushed her golden hair off of her face. "Those branches keep tugging at my hair, Rob. This is the absolute last straw. I'm telling you. Please remove this ugly old tree from our yard at once, Rob. I don't want to see it…"

"But, my dove," Robert took her ivory hands into his own. His new fiancée's fingers were rougher than Celeste's used to be, he noticed. *Rougher around the edges.* Lenore was certainly no fragile flower, but nor was her passion for the faint of heart. And, oh, how Robert was titillated to be wrapped around her finger.

"It provides shade for the delicate flowers, remember? Besides, it's merely a tree. What could it possibly…"

"I don't like it!" Lenore insisted, rolling her eyes to toward the clouds. "It's as simple as that. If you and I are to be married, I shall lay no eyes on this hideous thing blocking my view of the harbor from our bedroom."

"My darling, our bedroom would not even be facing this…"

"I don't wish to hear another word of it!"

EARTH UP YOUR ROOTS

Lenore folded her arms across her full chest. The pursuant quiet caused her to glance at Robert from the corner of her eye. A change of tactic was called for, she decided, in order to solidify her convincing.

Ever since she'd discovered his ex's little poetry engraved in the thick bark- signed by the initials she'd known to be her sister's- Lenore wished to have no remnant of the shameful past. A past that had caused her to lose a sister, in order to gain a wealthy husband. Desperate financial times upon the family had called for desperate measures.

Lenore raised the pitch of her voice and spoke through a sultry smile. "You do wish to have me happy in the bedroom, the living room, the kitchen, and in all the rooms with all the views we could enjoy each other's company for years to come…don't you, Robbie?"

"Alright, my darling," Robert sighed, clearing his throat. He was blushing, Lenore noticed. "I'll call my men first thing in the morning to take a look. They've got some sturdy axes and…"

He was caught midsentence when a particularly strong wind gust brought down the heavy thick branch atop his head at top speed. It was as if something had hurled it straight onto his skull.

"Rob!" he heard Lenore shriek as she rushed over to him with panic. But he could not even turn to see her beautiful countenance one last time before another woman's image appeared before his mind.

"You win, Celeste," Robert croaked in a whisper, looking up at the tree. Towering mighty before his fallen body. The branch that had just struck him was now raised in its usual position once again.

As his eyes closed to the world, he began regretting it all. The gradual poison he'd fed her nightly to expedite her death- albeit in a covert manner, of course. Had Lenore been worth it? God knew she'd been pressuring him to leave Celeste for the longest time, and he just hadn't had the heart.

Robert wasn't a monster. If he'd told Celeste he'd fallen in love with another woman-her very own sister, at that- surely, she would have succumbed to a quicker death through a heart attack, or even a more painful one through an actual cancer of some sort.

No. Robert couldn't allow for Celeste to hate him. It was a wonderful thing to feel- *being loved* by someone as much as she had. Yet what could he have done? He also wanted *to love*. And he simply could not feel any romantic affection toward Celeste. It'd been Lenore who'd stolen his heart. *Perhaps literally so*, was Robert Carlisle's last thought as he closed his eyes to the world.

§

Lenore wiped the single tear off her blushing cheek. Her sharp nails dug into her neighbor Michael's arms before her late fiancé's grave. What a kind neighbor Michael Thompson had been. *A well-off widower*. Lenore gazed into his eyes as the sermon continued, witnessed by several others- the identities of whom she could not quite make out at that moment.

Her and Michael were more appropriate for each other, Lenore supposed. *Perhaps this entire thing could have been destined-kismet-after all.* The thought brought a smile onto her face.

To be fair, Lenore had insisted that her mother-in-law-to-be bury him right by his favorite tree: the one he hadn't wished to cut down. *Poor Robert.* He should have listened to her.

Thank you, Celeste, Lenore thought, taking in a deep breath as she gazed at her late sister's engraving.

You've forgiven me, after all, I suppose, she smiled as the leaves almost whispered a soft agreement with her in the wind. *Causing this occasion by giving Robert what he deserved, I suppose, and allowing me to grow closer to Mr. Thompson.*

Lenore glanced at the luscious leaves shining in the sun. *I'll let you remain here after all, in return.*

- - - - - - - -

EARTH UP YOUR ROOTS

to wake each day on the battlefield
lacking weapons or a shield
against enemies both perceived and real-
both the green-eyed monster they never reveal
and the inner critic you attempt to conceal

no one is without fault
even if they've casted the first stone
discover the solace you seek in nature
discover the solace of what has been sown

                                in environments
                              where authenticity
                    can ignorantly be referred to
                            as 'mental illness'

                                an inauthentic self
                    being deemed 'appropriate'- meanwhile
                  can bring about actual mental ailments

    salvage your psyche: relocation and redirection
                              can-in one lifetime-
                            catalyze reincarnation

SELIN SENOL-AKIN

slice a poem

you'll find the dirt
underneath the charming verses
the blood
underneath a message that rejoices

the tears contributing to the floods
...and the heavy sighs to the flow
...blooms in secret, not allowed to grow

the silent screams
the hidden dreams

concealed pathways and dark rooms
unawareness of all that looms

slice a poem
and you'll find *reality*

...and there within lies the real beauty

EARTH UP YOUR ROOTS

BUD

some bruises are grapes
　　that simply cannot be turned into wine ...
　　　　best thriving left on their vine

SELIN SENOL-AKIN

a lovely home
can hide a million flaws
a beguiling smile
can scratch deeper than claws

some rule emptiness
situated on thrones
throwing only petals
while evading hurled stones

a broken vase
can struggle to keep the rose
sniffed but not rooted
only joy stems from prose

                        the most beautiful walls can hide
                        the most heartbreaking tragedies

                        plaster painted to look sturdy
                        vines wound to appear pretty

                all the while with the foundation- shaky-
                      accruing rooted, lethal maladies

                              a façade of dreams
                                    while
                          coming apart at the seams

EARTH UP YOUR ROOTS

nature fills our shoes
whilst we're occupied
in our daily ruse

rain waters the seeds
we tend to ignore
in our daily grind
whilst we're stepping on the earth's weeds
tending to man-made deadlines and deeds
paying no mind

climbing the corporate ladder,
or
watching the dandelions scatter?
which one is sadder?

I prefer the latter

SELIN SENOL-AKIN

THE RUBY

WITH THE SUNRAYS STINGING HER EYES stronger than usual that early autumn morning, Ruby Sternstein woke up to a curious mix of bird sounds and suburban construction projects in her Smithtown neighborhood.

Her wrinkly hands were adorned with rings. Her usual, even when sleeping. They held on tightly to the edge of the bed, where her silky pajamas had allowed her to slide herself up with ease.

My hair! Her Harold had adored it in curls. Ruby had to ensure they were still intact each and every morning. She squeezed her thighs as a massage- her right leg had particularly weakened over the past four decades. Wobbling toward her wooden vanity table, Ruby situated herself on the velvety-cushioned chair.

EARTH UP YOUR ROOTS

What she saw in the mirror nearly took her breath away, and she had to hold on to the corner of her armoire for dear life. So hard, in fact, that her perfectly lined-up row of peach and mauve lipsticks fell down to their sides- with one or two even rolling down to the musky-carpeted floor.

Before her, the silver ringlets on her head were now transformed in time to their once-chestnut hue, silky and gleaming in the sun with life. Ruby's staggering hand caressed her cheek, viewing the reflection display her once supple skin. With cheeks of rose-pink- she appeared to be closer to herself around age 30 rather than the current one of 70.

Her heartbeat grew speedier. What exactly was happening? Ruby closed her eyes and said a little prayer. *Blessed are you, our God, Ruler of the Universe, who is good and causes good. What I see before me- youth- is beautiful, but I am frightened. Please let this go away, please let this vision go away.*

She opened her eyes with hope, only to shut them again at the sight of her younger self reflecting back at her. *If only prayers came true in an instant,* she thought. Ruby had prayed every night for two years- never missing a single day, after Harold's accident- until eventually giving up. The tragic, heartbreaking car crash many of the locals continued to whisper about on the rare occasion they saw her walking about her front lawn. Tending to a random plant still hanging on to vitality, though Ruby and time itself had long given up on tending to them.

Crazy lady, she'd overhear the neighborhood kids say about her with chuckles- undoubtedly overhearing things from their cold-hearted parents. *Children, after all, are never inherently evil,* Ruby knew.

§

"Dylan? Oh, Dylan. My handsome son, I'm so happy you're visiting on this day out of all days?"

"What's the matter, mother?" Dylan pressed both of his firm hands on his mother's shoulders. "Is everything alright? Is it those damn opossums again? Because, you know I've been meaning to call the exterminator this week. Really, I have. But that latest client at the firm has been bugging us constantly about…"

"It isn't the opossums, Dylan," Ruby dismissed. She ran her fingers through his light, sandy hair- wavy like the Atlantic. *My handsome, lawyer son.* Why hadn't he gotten married with that girlfriend of his yet? She was probably delaying it, that foolish girl. Her son was quite the catch, as far as Ruby was concerned.

"Is it the raccoons, then, mother?" Dylan's hands were moving a mile a minute. The rate of his speech- even speedier. "Have they been stealing your gardenias again? Because you know…"

"Come with me upstairs to my bedroom," Ruby interrupted with a smile, linking her arm with that of her son's. "I want to show you something…"

"Ok, hold on tight, mother. Are you sure you don't want the stair-lifts to help you when I'm not around? It can be dangerous, you know, for you to …"

"There are more dangerous things for an

old lady living alone than navigating up and down stairs, my Dylan," Ruby went on, her toes inside thin velvet slippers- a shade darker than the color of her name- gripping on to each step for dear life. Her free arm was gliding up the handrail. The tone of her voice dropped. "More disturbing things, such as her foggy mind. Oh, I do hope I'm alright. But I saw it. I saw what I saw…"

"What did you see mother? When? Where?"

Ruby paused before the crème-colored wooded door with the brass doorknob. Her bedroom. She took in a deep breath. "In here…"

Ruby pushed the door slowly and placed a finger onto her lips. As if there were a class in session in the room she did not want them to interrupt. How she missed her teaching days. Harold had advised her against working once she'd become a mother.

She stood before the table with an abrupt halt to her lethargic strutting, pointing. "There!"

"Can you even make out your reflection in this aged thing, mother?" Dylan walked to the table and hunched downward, eyeing the glass with a quizzical countenance. "I'm afraid we might have to replace this..."

"It shows me what I need to see just fine, Dylan!" Ruby raised her voice, albeit it was quivering. She gasped, slowly cupping her hand over her mouth. "Oh, my dear Lord...."

She stared this time to see Harold hugging her from behind, placing a red-jeweled necklace around her neck.

"A ruby for my Ruby..." he was whispering in her ear. Fastening the necklace behind her neck with meticulous attention, he added a soft kiss on her neck in the way she liked- still giving her entire body goosebumps.

"Thank you." Ruby closed her eyes, allowing her smile-ridden face and head to lay backward toward her husband's sturdy chest.

"Mother!" Dylan suddenly called out, coming up behind her. His voice sounded to Ruby as if it could have been coming from the garden outside. "You were almost going to fall!"

"Nonsense, Dylan," Ruby chuckled, blushing as she turned around to face her son. "Your father's a strong man."

"Mother…please lay down. Rest a bit."

"Why didn't you welcome him- your father? Say hello! You certainly have been taught your manners, my boy."

"Who?" Dylan asked with a raised brow. "Mother? You really should sit down, and I'll get you some…"

"You don't see him? Oh, dear." Ruby blinked a couple of times. "Harry?" she whimpered to the mirror, smiling as he slowly returned it, appearing before her again. "There you are…"

"Uh, mother…."

"He's wearing his navy gentleman's suit," Ruby went on, cutting in. "Do you remember it? The one he adored wearing to special dinners. Come to think of it, Dylan- you should wear it. After your father takes it off, that is. You should borrow it. You have your father's build."

"I will," Dylan's voice accepted. He added a heavy sigh.

"Why don't you wear it to your special dinner tonight with Emma, actually?" Ruby threw a mischievous glance at her son from the reflection in the mirror. Her Harold had dissipated, though he could sense him there with his family still. *He must be avoiding calling further attention to himself*, Ruby decided. *We both know there's a more important matter at hand, with regards to our son.*

"My special dinner? Oh, right, right. Emma's birthday," Dylan's voice was lackadaisical.

Could it be that it was her *son* who'd needed more convincing? Could it have been Dylan who was to blame for their cold feet toward marriage, and not Emma's? Ruby rolled her eyes. What fools the couples of this generation were. No one was getting any younger.

§

"Ta da!" Dylan did a little spin for Ruby, throwing in an exaggerated, toothy grin at the end. "How do I look, mother?" He had decided in a manner of minutes to indulge her mother in her little hallucination before the mirror in her room, and had put on the navy suit he'd known his mother to have been referring to earlier. Her favorite one of his late father's. Hanging crease-free on his side of closet.

"It's perfect!" Ruby exclaimed, her palms folded together atop her chest. "We knew you'd be perfect in it!"

"Well, I'm honored papa has allowed me to wear it," he winked, adjusting the collar while caressing his mother's cheek. "I just have to make sure to spray on some cologne before I pick up Emma, though. Smells a bit like mothballs, and there's no time for dry cleaning…what's this?"

Dylan locked eyes with his mother, whom he saw to be smiling wider now as she observed her son placing his hands into the jacket's pockets. His hand gripped something hard, and took it out to see a classic-looking crème box in the left pocket. Dylan shed a tear. *Papa was left-handed, too.*

"What's inside, Dylan?" Ruby's voice quivered, yet Dylan could still glimpse a hint of a smile on her expression rather than shock. She placed her hand on her mouth as he opened the box. "Oh, my Adonai! That is the very red necklace I saw him place around my neck in the mirror!"

"It's…beautiful, mother," Dylan stammered. "This…I…well, why would this be in his pocket? Had he not given this to you?"

"I believe he must have intended to, my boy," Ruby's gaze became lost in the mirror once again. "He whispered to me, as he put it around a young version of myself I saw in the mirror. 'A ruby for my Ruby', he said." Ruby sat down on the foot of her bed, closing her eyes.

"It was lovely to see my younger self in the mirror. Now that I think of it, your Emma sort of resembles my younger self, Dylan…"

"Oh, my," Robert bent down on his knees before Ruby. "Didn't Papa get killed right before your anniversary? Mother, I think he'd been wanting to give you this…."

"Yes," Ruby smiled now through her tears. "But he could have appeared to me for all of these years had he still thought I should own it. I spent other anniversaries without him. So, no. No, that couldn't be it, dear son. I think…I *sense* he wants you to have it- something in addition to that little rock I saw you prepare to propose to Emma…"

"Mother, it was on sale," Dylan was shaking his head. "I was waiting until Christmas. When I knew more for sure whether it would be the right thing…"

"We give you two our blessing," Ruby interrupted. "Harold has always dreamed of growing old together in this house, with the sound of grandchildren, Dylan. Your career will not provide you with any of that coziness. Possessions- present or of the past- will only possess *us* if we hang on to them. The future is more important…"

"It's not just about your blessing, mother," Dylan started to say, only to grow quiet as he saw the suddenly-stern expression on his mother's face. He sighed. Dylan really did want to move into the grand house- with or without Emma. His apartment in the city wasn't doing it for him anymore. And if a marriage was the only way to keep his folks' support…

"Dylan?" Ruby's voice cut into his thoughts.

EARTH UP YOUR ROOTS

"I just meant...we couldn't take something so obviously special for you, mother," Dylan cleared his throat.

"You two will have more use for it with your lifestyle than your little old mother, my boy," Ruby chuckled softly.

§

Was that her late husband shaking his head at her in the mirror? Ruby kept her head held high. So what if she had to get a little creative to convince their son to finally form a family of his own already?

"Don't worry, Harold," Ruby assured the reflection, twirling her silver curls in the mirror. "I'll get it back from that Emma girl. Eventually. Being married to someone of Dylan's status...I'm sure she won't mind. Not at all."

SELIN SENOL-AKIN

THERESA

MEETING A SELF-PUBLISHED AUTHOR, deemed notable enough to be a dying young girl's last wish? Had the world turned upside down while she'd been asleep?

"Are you certain I am the author she wishes to see, before she passes on?" Rebecca Thompson had inquired that morning, lowering her voice. "I mean, you know, *if* she passes on, that is. I do certainly hope she will recover, the poor thing...."

"Yes, Ms. Thompson," the man on the other side of the phone had assured her, introducing himself as Brock Richardson from the local chapter of Make-A-Wish Foundation. "We confirmed with young Theresa by showing her your indie-author's page. Quite professional by the way. You did the design all by yourself? I'll have to check out your books myself sometime."

Rebecca had blushed, at once flattered and also relieved. Not many people knew of the 'indie author' label for self-published, independent authors such as herself. A route that left her with little financial benefit after all the marketing expenditure she had to make out of her own pocket- uncovered by her actual cut of royalties from sales- yet creatively in control and happy about the entire process nonetheless.

Brock Richardson. The tall man with the slicked back brown hair and wiry glasses was now smiling handsomely before Rebecca. *His name sounds like a character I could use in the next book*, she thought, mirroring him as he eyed her up and down. Taking him up on his invitation from earlier that day hadn't disappointed her thus far.

"I appreciate that, Mr. Richardson," Rebecca went on, ignoring the burning sensation from the crimsoning of her cheeks. "Please forgive my confusion on the phone earlier. Despite having been fortunate enough to obtain some dedicated readers through my social media presence, I'm not exactly- you know- a J.K Rowling or Stephen King. To be widely-known enough to have been able to reach this young reader. I'm surprised, yes, but don't get me wrong- also incredibly honored!"

"Call me, Brock," the man replied, ushering her to take a seat on the other side of his desk. "Ms. Thompson, I also happen to be

Theresa's personal therapist. We've been having a lot of conversations about her need for connections, actually. She wouldn't tell me where she first came across your book- it was in her backpack when her aunt dropped her off here for treatment- but I believe she's connected through the title bearing her own name. Not sure what the plot is about exactly, but I'm sensing some particular affinity with the main character…"

"I suppose that could be it…" Rebecca said, unsure if the smile she'd plastered on her face was capable of disguising her concern. She was hoping that this young leukemia patient, whom she was told was around 14 years old, was not terribly affected by the particular, dark story she'd written.

Rebecca had never considered the impact- positive or negative- any of her writing could have on anyone. She liked to believe she'd been able to formulate an image of an inspiring writer on her social media handle- motivating aspiring writers to write stories of their own, and for readers to merely be intrigued and entertained. She'd always been careful not to include erotic or violent material- Rebecca hated the impact of such material on youth, especially in movies and video games.

But a young teenager - a likely sensitive

one at that, with her illness- reading the story about a young girl's self-destruction? And coincidentally sharing her name, at that? What impact was a lesser-known author such as herself possibly having on an impressionable young reader?

"I really do want to read your book, though, Ms. Thompson," Brock cleared his throat. "Especially now that I've met you. I'd love to support you. Is it available for sale online?"

"It sure is, through most online retailers," Rebecca smiled, biting her lip. "And, please, call me Rebecca."

"Will do," Brock smiled, swaying his body back and forth.

"Well?" Rebecca raised her eyebrow. "May I see her now? Theresa is expecting me, is she not? And you do approve of this meeting, I take it, as her therapist?"

"Oh, yes, yes, of course," Brock shook his head rapidly. "Your Covid-test came back negative. As I've stated, we'll keep the meeting to an hour- supervised by myself from the adjacent room to listen for potential emotional triggers for her. However surely unintentional as they may be, you can understand I may- in such a case- need to come in with some excuse and change the topic…"

"Oh, yes, of course, of course," Rebecca nodded. She held up the palms she'd lain on her lap. "I'll do my best to stick to how I developed my love of writing and what kind of things she's liked reading about, as discussed. I know the impact of the human psyche on physiology."

"Thank you," Brock smiled. "Medically, her cancer hasn't gotten worse over the last two months she's been here. The chemotherapy has catalyzed some stability, though we're now seeing that a bone marrow transplant to replenish the damaged stem cells may be in order. A donor with the haploidentical form of an allogeneic transplant- one from a parent- would have been ideal. Sadly, it cannot be the case for Theresa since her aunt's filled us in on how she lost her folks in a tragic crash as a young child."

"I cannot even begin to imagine…" Rebecca folded her arms closer across her chest. Or maybe she could. She closed her eyes a beat longer than intended, nodding as Brock continued to speak.

Tessa.

The name ran across her mind and Rebecca has to fight back tears. The baby daughter she'd had to leave beyond as a young woman studying away from home, having been left pregnant by the bartender that'd crushed her heart and idealistic dreams about love. *How can a young girl grow up not knowing those whose seeds had sprouted her?* The daughter whose name had inspired her naming of her fictional protagonist- not wanting to jinx her life somehow by naming her in the same exact way. The girl she had to give up for adoption to a kind, childless couple in Florida before her parents back up in Boston could ever suspect anything upon her return. Had her adopted mother ever revealed the truth to Tessa? Would she be angry with Rebecca if she knew? Could she understand?

"Her oncologist has actually been thanking me, claiming the stability might be the pleasant byproduct of our uplifting therapy sessions- igniting vitality into her spirits and such. But, Rebecca…" Brock leaned in closer to her face, his coffee eyes piercing through her own. He lowered his husky voice even lower.

"I know that deep down- it's somehow your story which has been the catalyst. No siblings or many friends she's ever spoken of. Her aunt concurs my theory with each visit- it's this *story* that she clings to. Your novel has somehow become her lifeline."

Rebecca reminded herself to blink, letting out a deep breath. "Brock…that's a lot for me to take in. A major responsibility. I mean, my book; I'm honestly not sure if it's- I don't know quite how to word this- a *positive* enough influence on such a vulnerable young girl. It's not exactly a self-help book, you know? Nor some inspirational autobiography. It's a psychological thriller of a sort…"

"She reads it over and over," Brock shrugged. "Excitedly so, each time. It makes her smile. And we don't ever want to deny that to our patients. We did read some of the reviews. We were assured there were no horrific scenes, foul language or intense eroticism or anything like that that could potentially jeopardize…"

"Oh, no, no, of course not," Rebecca interrupted, folding her arms across her chest as she leaned back in the black swivel chair. "It's nothing like that. It just describes…well…a broken family, and a young girl's search for herself through her search for them. And now that you've told me a little about her life- I'm a bit concerned."

"Well," Brock stood up silently, eyeing the circular clock on the wall as he patted his palms across the desk. "I understand your concerns, but it will be Theresa's time for dinner soon. The nurses are strict with her schedule, and I don't want to take away from your time with her. You don't want to cancel on her, do you?"

"No, no," Rebecca cleared her throat, sitting up straight in her chair. "Of course not."

"Then let me take you to see her," Brock gently tapped her shoulder two times. "Rest assured that seeing you should only be a good thing for our sweet patient. She's truly a bright girl- an absolute delight to talk to. Just like yourself."

As the two of them walked closer before Room 202, Rebecca shook out her arms and put on a big smile. A melodic, soft voice muttered "Come in," in response to Brock's knocking, and the door opened to reveal a cheerfully-dispositioned girl with a blue beanie covering her bare head, dark eyes striking on her pale skin.

"Rebecca!" she exclaimed, grinning from ear to ear. "Oh, sorry. Ms. Thompson. Come sit, please. Look I'm sitting crisscross apple sauce! There's room for you at the foot of the bed. Can she please sit here, Brock? Please, oh, pretty please?"

Rebecca and Brock exchanged smiling glances. "What a sweetie pie you are, Theresa. It's my pleasure to meet my favorite reader! And of course, you can call me by my first name."

As Brock motioned for her to sit down in deed on her bed's edge, Rebecca did so, folding her hands on her lap.

"I'll be right outside if you girls need me," Brock stated gently, giving Rebecca a wink that felt supportive to her.

"You're finally here!" Theresa was swaying back and forth, her arms hugging a pillow on her legs. "I'm sure Brock's filled you in on how much I love your novel. I've read it three times!"

"Three times?" Rebecca gulped. *So, she has read the ending.* The ending that Rebecca had secretly wished this teenager somehow hadn't gotten up to when she'd decided, merely halfway through the book- perhaps on some youthful whim- that she'd enjoyed enough of the story to request meeting her.

"Yes! May we take a picture together, Rebecca?"

"A picture?" Rebecca stammered. "Oh, of course. I can take it on my phone and send Dr. Richardson. I'm sure he can…"

"They give me a cell phone, you know," Theresa rolled her eyes playfully. "I use it to chat with my support group mostly. Other kids across the country. Three back home in Florida, actually.

EARTH UP YOUR ROOTS

Come closer please- my arms can only reach so far for the selfie. The cancer is not contagious…"

"Aww, nonsense..." Rebecca dismissed with a nervous chuckle. *Florida.* She tried to push her own trigger words out of her mind, as the name of the state Rebecca herself had grown up in was mentioned. *Tessa.*

"It is not that, dear Theresa," she continued, edging herself closer to the young patient. "On the contrary, it is I who wouldn't to pass germs of any kind from the city life outside of this secluded space you've got out here…."

"It'll be alright," Theresa's eyes met hers. "Say cheese…"

Isn't this AC turned on a bit high? Rebecca rubbed her hands across her arms following their little photography session. She instinctively found herself reaching for the blanket she spotted hanging off the side of Theresa's bedside chair. "Put this across your shoulders, honey. It's chilly in here, aren't you cold?"

"You're right, I do get cold easier than usual these days," Theresa smiled, allowing Rebecca to place the navy-blue sheet across her shoulders. "Theresa in the book also got cold a lot, didn't she?"

Rebecca's stomach did a little drop. She plastered on a smile. "Yes. Yes, I suppose she did." For a moment, she had to fight the urge to let out a tear, staring there right into this young reader's eyes. *I wonder what it would have been like to raise a daughter.*

"I have a secret…" Theresa whispered, glancing toward the door before cupping her tubed hand around her mouth. "I *am* Theresa. *The* Theresa."

"Hmm?" Rebecca tried nonchalantly, despite a rapidly increasing heartrate. "Sorry, I didn't quite catch that…"

"This story, Ms. Thompson. I mean, Rebecca. This is my life. Well, *almost* to a T…. It's remarkable…"

"*Your* life…?"

"I keep thinking about what will become of me…" Theresa went on with a nod. "Since, so far in my life everything's come about as the chapters had happen to the 'Theresa' character in the book…I mean, except the part about her mother having left her and her dating the wrong crowd. I'm not even fifteen and sixteen yet like those chapters in the book. But I do wonder if I'll end up like the ending?"

"The ending…" Rebecca sighed. She closed her eyes. The character based half on her own life…where she'd purposely written in a twisted end for the character's father- literally- to creatively avenge the bartender who'd broken her heart and left her pregnant. The other half of the character had been based on the life of the one person she had long suppressed from her consciousness; how she'd long imagined her Tessa growing up, including a quarter of the details she'd known of or imagined from the daughter she'd given away. *It was for her own good.*

"I like to believe I purposely left the ending a bit open-ended," Rebecca forced herself to smile. "We see the tragic end her father faces, but I've left it up to the reader to decide if Theresa ever gets to meet her mother or not. I wanted to leave some room for hope, I suppose, after the rest of the book. I didn't want to have any regrets with a concrete ending…"

"Do you have any regrets, Rebecca?"

"Not really. I mean, I like to think that I've made the best decisions based on the options I had at a time throughout my life." *The baby I gave up for adoption.* Of course, Rebecca could never share that part with this young fan of hers. She'd certainly view her as a heartless monster, and her fantasy of a favorite author would diminish. Brock would call it a terrible mistake to make in the life of a cancer patient.

"Oh, come on…pleasssse" Theresa insisted in a sing-song voice with a wide-mouthed smile. "Just for cheeseeee."

Rebecca raised a curious eyebrow before breaking out into laughter. The bright young girl before her was still so childlike she could literally feel her heart melt. "Oh, alright. You're adorable. I really do feel chilly in here. So, hmm, a regret? Maybe I would say- not staying in Florida. I was studying at Florida State University in Tallahassee. Fell in love with the warmth and the general vibe of the place. I would have stayed if I could. I returned up here to the Northeast too soon."

"Why?" Theresa made a face of disgust.

"Oh, you know- let's just say it was a romantic heartbreak sort of situation. You'll understand when you're older. And you will, dear Theresa! I spoke with Brock- the doctors are saying you've been making such progress…"

"No," Theresa interrupted. "I meant- why would anyone love Tallahassee that much? I spent my entire life there-until Aunt Lucille took me up here last year for better treatment. It's the most boring…"

EARTH UP YOUR ROOTS

Aunt Lucille. As Theresa continued relaying tidbits from the 'boring' activities she took part in during her young life- Rebecca couldn't shake the name she'd just heard out of her mind. *Lucille.* Certainly, it couldn't be Lucille Phelps- wife of William Phelps- the adopted mother who had been staying in contact with her regarding how *her* Tessa was being raised, could it?

Her Tessa was a cheerleader, Lucille had relayed to Rebecca- a lithe athlete, even as a freshman in high school. *Her* Tessa was an avid horseback rider- with long, flowing brown hair in the video clips Lucille had sent her.

"Rebecca?"

"Oh, sorry," Rebecca attempted to return from her reverie and back to the curious-eyed girl before her. "I was just thinking back on a friend I had back in Florida. A woman named Lucille, just like your aunt."

"Where is she now?" Theresa asked.

"My daughter?" Rebecca asked in response.

"Your...who?" Theresa's voice quizzed. "You have a daughter?"

Shit!

"Hmm? Oh...um, Theresa," Rebecca held out an imploring finger, walking toward the door.

"Could you excuse me for a moment? I have to have a word with Mr. Richardson- I'll be right back. I promise…"

"I was asking about the friend named Lucille you mentioned. But, Rebecca- you have a daughter? That's so cool! I don't remember reading about it in…"

"Just a moment…" Rebecca's quivering hand had to struggle a bit with the door handle, yet she was able to step outside and into the adjacent lobby area where she knew Brock Richardson would be waiting, listening to their recorded session from his smart phone, headphones on.

She spotted him walking toward her. "Brock, I…"

"Ms. Thompson, you mentioned something about a daughter to young Theresa?" Brock's voice was stern. He was shaking his head. "I'm glad you stepped out. I was just thinking of a way to come inside, actually."

"Brock, I…I mean, Mr. Richardson. It was a slip of the tongue. I wanted to ask you, if you don't mind, the patient's aunt's full name, if I may?"

"We are not allowed…" Brock continued. "Ms. Thompson. I'm sorry- I feel we may be in need for a more thorough discussion, perhaps, of young Theresa Phelps' background- but not now. You left her in there before your hour was up. She must be feeling so confused. May I please suggest going back in there and at least rounding up the discussion with something about the writing process or...."

"Phelps?" Rebecca whispered with a crack in her voice, placing her palm across her mouth. "As in Lucille and William Phelps?"

"Rebecca...." Brock placed his arms softly on her shoulders. *He called me Rebecca again.* "My God...Did you do background research on your young reader, after all, or something? How did you know the full names of Theresa's aunt and her husband?"

"Brock..." Rebecca shook her head subtly side to side. "No. I had no idea who this reader was before today. I swear to God. And Lucille and William are the twosome who adopted my daughter from me in Florida, before I went back up to Boston to my family. I was a young woman. After a mistake...and..."

"Theresa's parents- adopted or real- are passed, as far as we know..." Brock shook his head, puzzled.

"No, no! Lucille and William are perfectly alive, and living down in Tallahassee, raising my daughter they adopted when she was a baby…"

"Rebecca…could you kindly tell me more about this daughter of yours?" Brock guided Rebecca's arm downward as they both sat in the lobby chairs. A couple of onlookers shot them dirty looks. "Really briefly and quietly, please. We could discuss this further in my office later, but I don't want to keep Theresa waiting too long…"

"It's a long story. I was too young to raise my Tessa. My parents would have absolutely disowned me had they learned I'd gotten pregnant while living away for college. It was the best I could do…"

"Tessa?" Brock asked loudly. He took in a deep breath and lowered his voice. "When was your daughter born?"

"Brock…no...you can't possibly be implying…"

"When was her last birthday, dear author? Just curious? Come on! A parent always knows his or her kid's birthday. I sure as know my own girl's birthday! And, yes, you can bet your bottom dollar I sure as heck am asking because I know certainly when we here at the clinic all celebrated Theresa's birthday last…"

"May…"

EARTH UP YOUR ROOTS

"May…?"

"May 25th!"

Brock stayed silent for an entire hour- at least that's how long around a minute or so felt like for Rebecca.

"Please say something Brock…" she managed to get out through falling tears.

Finally, he spoke. "This 'aunt' that visits Tessa; I don't believe she's been wholly honest with us. Or your daughter's adopted mother with you. I'm beginning to think they may even be the same woman. So much mystery here. About her identity, and the crash, and …heck, now I'm seeing maybe it wasn't coincidence this 'aunt' has given her your book…"

"When is *Theresa's* birthday, Mr. Richardson?" Rebecca asked, enunciating each word. "You called her Tessa just now. I'm sure it was a slip of the tongue…Right? Right?"

"May 25th…" Brock's gaze was fixated on the floor. He chewed on his lips. "Theresa was just the nickname she's asked us to call her by. *Tessa* Phelps was born in 2008. Sound familiar?"

"Yes," Rebecca whimpered, eyes closed. *Too familiar*. "When's this *Lucille* coming to see you next? I'd like to be here as well. I'd like to know whose pictures she's been sending me, saying they're of my daughter…"

"Can I see those pictures?" Brock asked, reaching out his hand. "Please?"

"Oh my God…," he continued, after Rebecca had given into his insistence and shown him the photos from her smartphone. "Lucille's been sending you *my* daughter's photos and videos. Mary- my ex…She shares Maddy's photos all the time on social media. I warned her! I always warned her…"

"Brock…" Rebecca interrupted. There was a matter of life and death, she'd realized- more urgent at that moment than unraveling the mystery before them. "If she's really… *my* Tessa in there. Then maybe…there's a chance for her? For that- parent donor you'd lost hope on?"

"Yes" Brock smiled through tears. He took her hands in his. "I'm beginning to see that too, now. Yes."

- - - - - - - -

EARTH UP YOUR ROOTS

dependent flora
ornamental
wait for their roots
to be watered-
fundamental

to be nourished by
nature
if not a human
caretaker

they can rot:
they're prepared
for their lot

dependent humans
need nourishment
from one another

a friend, a lover
a sister or brother

must too prepare for
their fate
watering may not
arrive
at an expected date

what differentiates
us
from the plants
is a better ability
to earth up
our own dents

everyone mourns
the dead
until they forget…

appreciate-
while alive-
the chances to refresh
you still have, yet

promises spoken
bad habits unbroken

not recognizing a king or a queen
while so used to the routine

exposing your heart
pain disguised as art

life is already rough
if you're soft while they're tough

my diamond in the rough
say 'enough is enough'

EARTH UP YOUR ROOTS

REAP

we cannot BUILD
with a small 'u' and capital 'I'
or a capital 'U' and small 'i'

as equals
love grows

SELIN SENOL-AKIN

you've weathered the storm
surprised to have remained warm
they worshipped tiles and sheltered their hearts
while transparent vulnerability
like glass
was *your* norm

the lightning passed and only remained the
showers
your authenticity your umbrella- you didn't know
your powers

uproot if you must, but replant immediately
seeds need planting and stability- don't disrespect
serenity

nourish your seeds, and soon you'll grow flowers
even if the soil has pebbles, a home empowers

EARTH UP YOUR ROOTS

observe
the tree branches
like those of our lungs

one births sources of oxygen
the other utilizes to enrich lives

like the brain-shaped walnut
good for our thinker

or the eye-shaped carrot
good for our seeker

interdependence
is nature's silent reminder

without one another
living things
could neither blossom nor thunder

SELIN SENOL-AKIN

THE ROSE MOON

1952

WITH THE BREATHTAKING THRACIAN PLAINS growing more visible by the minute, Mehtap couldn't contain her excitement. "We're lucky, Elmas," she smiled at the young daughter seated beside her, the little hand sticky from clutching her own for over an hour now. Her daughter had just opened her eyes from a lengthy nap. "Your grandmother didn't quite have this comfort when she and her mother were expelled to Türkiye from Filibe[3]."

"When will *anneanne* return from her trip to Bursa?" Elmas inquired, rubbing her eyes-half-shut with the glare from the sunshine. "She'll be meeting up with us once we're in Istanbul, won't she?"

"You want your grandmother to tell you stories from my younger days again, don't you?" Mehtap asked with a mischievous wink. "Or

---

[3] The Turkish name for the city of Plovdiv in Bulgaria

better yet, her own stories…" At 45, she was told she still had looked to be at least ten years younger.

Her husband, Ali, had insisted she make the dangerous journey for the unification of their family. Originally from Sivas, he'd found work in Istanbul. "My people feel more comforted in the blend of this bigger city," he'd told her, referring to his status as a minority in the Turkish lands- being a non-Sunni, Alevi Muslim man. "But no place can quite feel like home if you and Elmas can't be with me. Besides- it seems it isn't going to be much safer for you two in Bulgaria."

The newly-victorious Communist regime had been expulsing as many Muslims as it could in an effort to 'cleanse' the country, and it had only been bringing the tales her mother would tell her from her own youth more vivid in her mind. The tales of similar expulsions and forced-conversions to Christianity by a country that had newly acquired its independence from the Ottoman Empire.

"Well, sure," Elmas' expression turned quizzical in an instant. "But I was just wishing she'd bring back more of those candy chestnuts."

"Why you little *kestane şekeri* yourself…" Mehtap tickled, causing both of them nearly lose their balance.

She knew she could have revealed her Christianity to the government in Bulgaria- half of her wasn't Turkish by blood, after all. She would then perhaps have been able to be spared the atrocities she'd begun to hear were being faced by the other Turks back in Bulgaria.

But Mehtap had secretly been glad to be inside Turkish borders again. Perhaps she could arrange to travel to Kars, as her mother had once taken her to as a little girl. Perhaps she could get more answers. Feel more fulfilled. And allow Elmas to meet the land and culture of her grandfather by blood.

§

1905

"Gülay," Ceyhun's azure eyes were sparkling in the sun. He held out his hands in a performing fashion. "*Sen güldün, ay güldü. Sen güldün, gönlümün bahçesine güller açtı. Sakın solma...*"

"Oh, Ceyhun, *ilahi*," Gülay blushed, placing her hand over her pink lips with a giggle. She gave him a small round of applause regardless. She'd grown accustomed to the neighbor boy's romantic poetry, using the 'rose' and the 'moon' references of her given name. His pushiness had always made Gülay's eyes roll toward the sky. They were only fifteen years old. What did Ceyhun- or she, for that matter- know about love?

"I have to go, Ceyhun. I promised *anne* I'll pick up some *kashkaval*[4] for our breakfast tomorrow. But I'll see you for dinner. Mother said we accepted your mother's generous invitation- I can't wait to eat her delicious *yaprak sarması* and *börek*. Mom refuses to accept that hers just aren't as delicious!"

"Oh, we can't wait, Gülay'ım," Ceyhun smiled. "I helped mother wrap those grape leaves with my own fingers- just for you!"

"Görüşürüz"!" Gülay waved him off, walking faster toward the market. Her mother, Ayşe, had indeed sent her to the market- just not for cheese, but rather for Swiss chocolates she insisted they take as a gift to dinner.

There were two markets in town- her mother would always tell her to go to the one owned by 'Ahmet amca', although the other one had been closer to their house. The one owned by a man named 'Hrant' she'd known to be of Armenian origin- mostly from his last name ending with '-*yan*'. That, and also from the way

---

[4] a yellow cheese common in Balkan communities

her mother and their neighbors would always warn her against visiting it, of course.

"What do we have against Armenians, mother?" she'd ask.

"Nothing, my love," Ayşe would answer her. "My favorite jewelry lady is an *Ermeni,* as you know, as is my hairdresser-Anoush. It's not us that has something against them- it's the other way around nowadays!"

"What do you mean?" Gülay had pressed her mother one time when they'd been having tea with Ceyhun and his mother, Sevil. Both of their fathers hadn't been around much, and this had bonded both the children as well as their mothers.

For the life of her, Gülay simply couldn't comprehend why residents of the same region- who'd been getting along well together for as long as she knew- would suddenly not like each other.

"Ever since the Russian uprisings began earlier this year, we hear there has been fighting between Armenians and Tatars over there…"

"So? We're not Tatars, mother," Gülay had shrugged.

"No, but Tatars are of Turkic origin," Ayşe had continued. "And some Armenians have begun to gossip that the Sultan may have been in support of them in Russia too…Mostly Russian-backed gossip, of course."

"That's absurd, *anne*," Gülay had rolled her eyes. "Who cares what some sultan did or thought? *Ermeniler* are our friends and neighbors here. We are all a part of the same empire…"

"A crumbling empire," Sevil had interjected, cutting her *dolma* dish as Ceyhun had returned her smile. "You'd be surprised at the paranoid things people would do and think as loss of power lingers nearer and nearer as a possibility."

Ever since he was a little boy, Ceyhun had been by his mother's side like a little pet. How Gülay had thought it childlike. And to think? Her friend Arzu had suggested he'd wanted to marry her!

The thought made Gülay shake her head- her flowing russet waves appearing almost golden in the glistening, August sunlight. She returned to the present moment, and decided to try to see what the big deal would be if she had decided to go to Hrant amca's bakkal, after all?

§

"Kimse yok muuuu....?" Gülay dragged out the end of her question, pushing the creaky wooden door further in. The market appeared empty of any human inhabitants, yet the plethora of fresh fruits and vegetables in crates were inviting to Gülay. *My mom has got to shop here more,* she thought. The produce in this novel market to her smelled better than the weekly street *pazar*[5] they'd often stock up at.

The lights were turned on, and Gülay thought she heard someone or something lurking about in another room behind a door adjacent to the main wooden counter. "Hello? I-um- was just looking for some chocolates, if you have…"

"Only the best ones!" the voice of a young boy around her age- smiling confidently despite his rather disheveled, uncut hair- took Gülay by a surprise. He closed the door behind him. "My father is at church. Sorry- I didn't hear you come in. Chocolates, you said?"

"Oh, alright," Gülay stammered, feeling heat on her cheeks after realizing the boy's eyes were fixated on her. She diverted her gaze to the apples situated before her. "No problem. Um- yes- those famed chocolates from Switzerland. Good ones. If you have. Which you said you did.

---

[5] Outdoor bazaar

So, yes. Special ones for guests. I love chocolates, don't you?"

Gülay focused on the boy's eyes again, noting his lingering smile despite his silence. What a fool she was! To ramble on about chocolates like that.

"You can have an *okka* for 50 *kurus*[6]…"

"Alright, thank you," Gülay managed to state, eyeing the boy's lean yet sturdy, tanned arms scoop some to wrap for her. Something from his upper arm- peeking underneath his gray top caught Gülay's eye as she placed the coins on the counter. A drawing of some sort?

"What's that?" she asked, intrigued beyond herself.

"What's what?" the boy asked, handing her the packet of sweets. His eyes followed where Gülay's had been focused. "Oh, my *dajvatsk*."

"Your what?" Gülay raised her brow.

"My tattoo," the boy smiled, rolling his sleeve further up to reveal the outline of a full rose. "You like it?"

"I do," Gülay smiled. "I like flowers. My own name means a flower. Well, partly. Gül-as a matter of fact. What a coincidence- right? It means a rose…" *I am an idiot.* She just wanted to

---

[6] Measuring units- for weight and currency, respectively

run home and throw herself on her bed in embarrassment.

"Gül? Is that your name? My name's Tigran," the boy reached out his hand.

His smile simultaneously managed to excite her and yet calm her nerves at the same time. "Gülay," she shook his hand. "Nice to meet you."

"Gülay…Gülay…" Tigran scratched his chin. "Not necessarily your name- but your face. Why do you look so familiar to me for some reason?"

"Well, we are seemingly neighbors," Gülay shrugged. "And my mother has been supporting my studies. I go to *Istanbul Kız Lisesi*. It doesn't allow boys, of course, but perhaps you've seen me around there?"

"You mean- glimpsing you, perhaps- while I was sneaking around there to check out girls or something?" Tigran let out a hearty laugh. "Armenian boy must be doing so to corrupt nice Muslim girls, is that it?"

"Wait- what!?" Gülay placed her arms on her hips. "I said no such thing! I just meant… I don't- you know- go around anywhere else much except school. And you appear around fifteen years old like me…"

"Or, is it that I must not be getting an education in secondary school myself, being an outcast with my tattoo and all. Is that it?" To Gülay's joy, Tigran's face appeared to be teasing her only.

"No, I didn't think that at all," Gülay raised her chin in defiance. "You actually sound quite well-spoken- with the intelligence of a fox, in fact, with these things you're throwing at me here, Tigran."

Tigran. Why had simply saying his name aloud rushed a flow of blood to her nether region all of a sudden?

"Well, I am fifteen, but, in any case- no, I don't believe I could have seen you anywhere else except today…" Tigran shrugged, his smile still on his face. "We just moved here from Kars…My mother and I, I mean. My father has had this market established for three years now, as you must know. You come here often?"

"Oh, yeah," Gülay fibbed. "All the time. Best vegetables in town!"

"Hmm, yet you weren't too sure about our chocolates, huh?" Tigran smirked.

"Well, I just never had the occasion to require chocolates," Gülay began, hands flying in the air in a multitude of directions. "I mean, my mother and I go often to visit *Sevil teyze* where

Ceyhun and I often try to play chess. But you know. We don't really get her chocolates or anything. Usually, my mother cooks something to take over there, but she's been tired lately, and…"

"I get it. You and this Ceyhun kid must have some special friendship," Tigran moved his eyebrows up and down.

"No, no! He's like a brother! Trust me!"

"I trust you…" Tigran winked.

"So, thank you for the chocolates," Gülay managed to get out after a deep breath. "Welcome to Istanbul. I hope to see you and *Hrant amca* around here again soon. You said he's your father, right?"

"Yes. And Where's your father, Gülay?"

"He, umm, is in the military. He doesn't live with us…"

"Oh, yeah?" Tigran's voice turned serious. "My aunt back in Kars recently wrote that several local Turkish fathers have gone to Tblisi to join the Tatars."

"What? That's absurd!" Gülay yelled. "How could you believe such lies without any knowledge? Through just gossip?"

"You said he's a military man, didn't you?" Tigran continued in a steady, calm voice. "It'd figure he'd fight to support other Muslims instead of our side…how else do you explain his absence? And why are you getting so defensive?"

"He left us for another woman!" Gülay blurted, sprouting tears. "Okay? Happy? Satisfied? Not for some stupid war! Not in anything against any of your people. Nothing but a man leaving his wife- and daughter, too- to go live with someone else in more comfort! Alright?"

"Gülay, I'm so sorry…" Tigran inched closer to her, shaking his lengthy black hair strands off of his face. "I really didn't mean to bring up such a sad topic."

"My mother was right…" Gülay muttered under her breath, unable to meet Tigran's eyes.

"About what!?" Tigran raised his voice.

"I shouldn't have come to this market!"

"Oh, because we're Armenian?"

"No, because you don't like *us*! How did I just meet you and you managed to make me cry, already?"

"Maybe we simply affected each other…" Tigran's voice said, even softer now.

"I have to go…" Gülay inched closer to the wooden door.

"Gülay, don't go, wait up…come back into the store. My dad makes good tea. It's fresh."

"No…"

"You don't drink tea?" Tigran raised his brow.

"Not much."

"How am I more Turkish than you?" Tigran snickered. "All you Turks are supposed to love your little tea in the little glass cups, aren't you?"

"For your information, I prefer fruit juice," Gülay crossed her arms, wiping her tears. "Freshly squeezed. Besides, tea and coffee are more for adults," she tossed back her long hair. "But then again, I'm talking to a young boy with a tattoo! Like an adult! An actual tattoo! How did your father allow for this?"

"Psst...he didn't," Tigran winked. "It's not exactly sinful or anything, like I know it is for you Muslims. But he still doesn't approve. So, I had to get it secretly. This woman friend I had…French…very professional. Always helped me with novel…experiences."

The look on his face had Gülay discern his implication at once. "Yuck! Gross. You had sex with a prostitute, didn't you?"

"It is a custom...all young men do it. And I *am* a young man, Gülay. Not some virgin boy. Like your Ceyhun, I imagine." He added with a smirk.

EARTH UP YOUR ROOTS

"Leave Ceyhun out of this," Gülay placed her hands on her hips. "We're all in the same grade! I'm leaving... I guess I'll see you around soon."

"You're welcome to stop by our store any time," Tigran placed his hand in his pockets. "For chocolates....or just for someone to have fun with to fight. But, hey- *all is fair in love and war.*"

Gülay crossed her arms. "Hmph! What did you do- read Shakespeare, or something?"

"That is a sixteenth century poet named John Lyly, Turkish girl," Tigran snickered. "As I was saying- *do* stop by again. It really looks like I can teach you a thing or two, now. We can even read together..."

"You...tattoo boy... *read?*"

"I can read you." With his hazel eyes locking themselves on her own amber ones- a minute longer than Gülay would otherwise have been uncomfortable with from anyone else. She found herself unable to leave.

"Oh yeah? And what do you read?" she asked.

"Our life story...I don't need to see your palm like the gypsies on the street," Tigran leaned closer to her face, placing one hand on the door behind her. "We are going to become very good friends. Very close, in fact. Friends with love. You will see."

"I'm …going home. It was nice to meet you, Tigran."

"Enjoy the chocolates, Turkish rose," he winked.

Who does he think he is? Gülay's mind was racing as she ran toward her home. What did Tigran know about love? A voice inside her said he'd probably know much more than Ceyhun.

Gülay snickered but stopped in her tracks soon afterward. The part that had begun to scare Gülay was the subsequent thought in her mind, as she inched closer to her house to accompany her mother for dinner at Ceyhun's house.

The thought that her whole being- her titillated mind, palpating heart as well as the throbbing wetness that had surprised her in his presence- was telling her; she *wanted* him to teach her love. The joy, the pain- all its forms.

Gülay could not wait to purchase chocolates from Hrant's market again.

§

1915

"Are you ready boy?"

EARTH UP YOUR ROOTS

"Yes, let's go uncle," Tigran replied. He looked around the trenches.

"The uprising will not be in vain…" his uncle continued, fixing his gun firmer on his belt. "The Russians are right. We deserve our own land here in this portion of the empire too. *Ararat* mountain belongs to our people! The Turks love claiming everything as their own."

"Yeah," Tigran smirked. *Like Ceyhun*. The man who'd married the only girl he ever loved. His Turkish rose- his Gülay.

How giddy they'd been for those precious two years, sneaking out of their homes to meet…making love at any opportunity they could. Until that fated day, behind the train tracks- when her mother caught her, and forbid them from seeing each other. And that Ceyhun had married her for her 'honor'.

Himarut'yun![7] Tigran had known the real reason. It was for her to get over him and marry a Muslim man instead. Over a decade had passed, and he could still smell her hair- sweeter than the flower after which she was named.

---

[7] An expletive in Armenian

1952

"*Anneanne,* you're back from Bursa," Elmas smiled at her grandmother.

"I know why you're really kissing me, *minik kuş,*" Gülay chirped. "Mehtap, you really have to cut this girl's hair. It's growing so thin-you have to let it grow thicker…"

"Mother! Please leave me be! I am a grown woman, and can decide for my own daughter, thank you very much!"

"Alright…" Gülay shook her head with a smile at her daughter. She tied the ends of her headscarf tighter underneath her chin. "Speaking of a woman making her own decisions…there's something I'd like to announce to you, my girls. After Ceyhun's death, you are the only two people I have left in this whole world… And I do hope you can visit. But… I have decided to move out East. I will live out the rest of my remaining days in Kars!"

"Kars?" As little Elmas asked her mother where her grandmother would be going, Gülay closed her eyes and smiled at the memory. That day on the trenches in Kars, where she'd insisted to Ceyhun she'd wanted to teach English.

"Our life story…" She could still hear the sound of his teenaged voice when she'd first met

EARTH UP YOUR ROOTS

him at his father's market, nearly 50 years ago. Tigran had told her he could 'read' their story. He'd referred to them being as one- coupled up- though they had just met. Had he had powers to foresee the future?

Her mother, Ayşe, would smirk at such things, chastising her for saying such things were not *caiz*[8].

If he had indeed seen their future- would he have done it all over again? Or would he have left the Turkish girl who'd entered his family market that summer alone, instead?

A single tear dropped on her cheek, and her granddaughter, Elmas, looked at her with sympathy. She yanked her mother's arm for attention, as they both looked back at Gülay. Mehtap did indeed catch her mother's eye and asked if she was alright.

Gülay smiled and nodded, but in her heart- she knew Mehtap had sensed what she'd been thinking. She was long told the identity of her father. Gülay had had many regrets- but loving Tigran, and carrying his child as a fruit of their love had never been one of them. The child that would have certainly had her on the streets had her friend Ceyhun not sacrificed his own

---

[8] Permissible according to Quranic law

conservative ideals in a woman for his love- and married her immediately after finding out about her condition. He'd been gracious to pass Mehtap off to their families and circle as their own, following a swift marriage ceremony.

1915. That year of her Kars visit. Ceyhun had called her 'crazy' to do so, but she'd insisted it was even more noble to educate the children in such a volatile region. She'd witnessed his body dying. It'd been years since they hadn't seen each other- yet there they were. It'd been fated for them to be together at least in death, Gülay knew.

A crescent moon had now been tattooed next to the rose- she stroked it as he'd recognized her and rolled up his sleeve. She'd given the tattoo a kiss, right before doing so on his dying lips as well. He had reached his hand across her face and whispered her name whilst she'd stroked his tattoo- now of her full name.

"We're yours, Tigran…" she'd whispered. "Mehtap and I…Always yours."

Tigran had nodded, closing his eyes with a satisfied smile as he took his last breath, his head falling back on her hand while Gülay laid it gently onto the blood-streaked ground.

- - - - - - - -

EARTH UP YOUR ROOTS

THE DRIVER

MARCO RAMIREZ SQUINTED TO SEE through the foggy window, the rain pounding the glass stronger than his heartbeat did so through his chest. "Oh man, I've gotta get these slow-ass wipers fixed before they remove my Lyft eligibility."

He eyed the alert on his phone from the corner of his eye, signaling to switch to the right lane. 'Delilah'. Two miles down.

"Damn…" he muttered aloud. The customer had chosen the more expensive ride option rather than waiting a bit longer. "This lady must be in a hurry."

Whatever. Marco needed the money. The summer camp his wife had had her eye on for their son came at a hefty price- just for three lousy weeks of painting and dancing. Something about steeper prices due to less kids being allowed. *Damn coronavirus restrictions.*

He halted the car upon spotting a rather plump woman with an attractive face framed by rain-soaked black hair pulled up in a bun. She was holding the hands of a little boy around his Peter's age. She had on a yellow coat that was easy to spot.

"Good evening, ma'am. How are…"

"Please, just drive," her voice interrupted him in a panic- loud, even from behind her pale blue mask. "Scooch over, come on!"

Marco noticed the boy's slumped shoulders and sullen, brown face. He didn't protest as he wriggled his body toward the corner of the seat. "Okay ma'am, just tell the boy to keep his mask on, please. It's the company rules…"

"We left very fast…no mask…" the woman's voice was stern. "Can't you see he's been crying? Because of my husband…just please, let's go already!"

"Oh, okay," Marco saw through the window reflection just then that this 'Delilah' lady had something red on her cheeks. Lipstick she had put on haphazardly, perhaps? *No. Blood!*

Oh, shit! Marco thought. Had her husband beaten her or something? "Ma'am, are you alright?"

"I'm trying to be, thank you," she replied with a sigh, adding quickly in exasperation.

"Please, just drive...We need to get away, now..."

Mami! Ay Dios mio! No, papi, por favor, détente! The image of his drunken father slapping his mother before his six-year-old self flashed through Marco's mind just then.

A loud car speeded by, allowing him to reconnect to the present. "Idiot! Speeding through the rain like that! Sorry, Ma'am. Please excuse my language."

"That's alright. Some people don't care about endangering others..."

Marco noted the woman was staring out the window. "Would you like me to take you somewhere...special? You know, where workers can help victims in your position...?"

"What do you know of my position?" she barked.

"Sorry," Marco held out a hand to the mirror so that the passenger behind him could see, the other still on the steering wheel. "You're right, you're right. I just want you to know you have options, and that, you know- you and the boy can be safe."

"The address we're heading to is the one place he'll never dare go to find us," Delilah's voice stated, calmer now despite the smirk on her face. "Believe me."

"Alright, ma'am, we're almost there." Marco glimpsed his phone- mere minutes were indeed left of the ride. A distinct text message tone alerted his attention back to his phone from the road. He caught snippets of the notification as he drove.

Child abduction. East Hills Police.
Victim: Pedro Ramirez, 12 years old, 5 ft, short black hair, last seen wearing a Knicks jacket
Suspect: Delilah Gomez, 34, 5 feet 5 inches, 160 lbs., long black hair, last seen wearing a yellow jacket and matching rain boots

Marco's hands began to tremble as he cleared his throat, whistling a tune as the notification disappeared. *Mierde.*

"Are they expecting flooding?" the woman asked him. He met her intense gaze from the mirror. "Sounded like a weather emergency alert."

Marco took in a deep breath, glancing at the boy's shiny navy-blue jacket, with orange block-letter writing that read 'New York'. He wasn't much of a basketball man, but he had a pretty good feeling that had been the logo and coloring for the Knicks. "Nah, I doubt it, ma'am," he responded as calmly as he could. "They always exaggerate in 'em weather alerts, you know what I'm saying?"

"You saw the message, didn't you-*Marco*?" Something about the way she pronounced his name shook Marco to his very core. And just how could she have known his name? *Oh, right- Lyft displays our names and car information.*

"What do you mean?" he managed.

"I'm not stupid, Driver. Shit! I can't believe the bastard survived to fucking issue an alert..."

"He's alive!" the boy spoke excitedly and for the first time. He wiped the silent tears that had drenched his face.

"You shut your mouth!" the woman warned him in a quiet but stern voice, placing a finger on her lips.

Survived? Had this woman been the one to try to hurt that man? His mind raced to his Uncle Juan and his crazy wife, Maria; Marco knew violence didn't only pertain to male perpetrators.

"Are you driving to Exit 37 or not?" Delilah stormed, interrupting his ponderings. "I paid for your services, you're obliged to take me to Roslyn..." Delilah flashed what looked to be the corner of a large kitchen knife from the corner of her handbag, holding it high toward her chest in a way that was visible to Marco.

Crazy bitch!

"Oh, of course, of course, ma'am," Marco knew he had to play smart if he wanted to survive another day to hug his son and wife again. "I…I was just worried about the crying boy you've got there with you. Other than that- yeah, I received the message, but it's none of my business. We never know what goes in a private domestic situation. It's just my job to drive. Please, relax…relax…It's okay…"

"I suppose you're going to tell me to trust you or something now, aren't you?" Delilah quipped, adding a little laugh. "I can never trust a man. I did once- and look where it's gotten me. On the run from the cops, accused of kidnapping my own son- by a man whom I had to fight off in self-defense…Of course, he has to go and twist it against me. Trust a man…Bah!"

"Self-defense," Marco nodded rapidly. He looked at his phone again- one minute was left. *Thank God.* "Yes, of course, I understand."

He took another glance at the boy. His face was now looking to him like a physical mixture between his son Peter's as well as Marco's own younger self.

Papi, no!

EARTH UP YOUR ROOTS

Could Delilah have been telling the truth? Could she really have been a victim of domestic violence who simply had to fight back in order to protect the life of both herself and her boy.

Gomez. The woman did have a different last name than Pedro. Then again, he knew women had not always taken their husband's last names- if they were even married at all, that is, which this woman had earlier implied she was.

Marco saw that Pedro was eyeing him curiously- not shying away when he caught it in the mirror. This woman wasn't particularly very warm with him either. Criminal or not, he was hoping Delilah would be a satisfied-enough customer to leave him alone once he drove away from their destination. That knife in her bag certainly wasn't the last image he wanted to see before closing his eyes to this world.

Nothing was making sense to Marco any more as he pulled up to a one-story, white-brick private house very close to the exit. A small, rather run-down front lawn displayed a couple of gnomes, and little else. Something about the place was looking familiar to him, but Marco couldn't quite put his fingers on it.

"Goodnight, ma'am," Marco feigned a smile, turning genuine when he looked at Pedro getting out of the car. "Stay safe, Pedro." The boy smiled.

Was it foolish of him to use the child's name that he'd read from the alert? *Oh, what the hell.* Delilah had already known about Marco's newly-acquired knowledge.

As an elderly woman treaded toward them from the front door of the house, Delilah didn't utter a word. She shut the door behind her.

Marco clicked the locks and was just about to speed away when he heard *her* voice. That all-too-familiar, warm, high-pitched voice, coming from the elderly lady whose face was becoming clearer now as day as she came out of the shadows of the evening, and closer to the street light to welcome Delilah and Pedro.

Marco opened his door at once, and got his body outside. *"Mami?"* Tears rolled down his cheeks as a million thoughts sped through his mind at once. The knife! Was his mother in danger?

Hugging? What was his mother- whom he'd known to be in her Florida home- doing in Long Island? Embracing these people- one of whom was just listed as a kidnapping suspect on an Amber alert, for Christ's sake?

"Ma!" He turned off the ignition and got

out of the car fully this time. Finally, the woman's ears heard him.

"*Mi hijo!*" his mother put a hand around her mouth, the other still around Pedro. Delilah turned to shoot Marco a confused glare. "*Mi guapo hijo!* You guys have met?

"Met?" Marco walked toward them slowly. "How do you know these two, *mami*? And what are you doing up here in New York? You didn't tell us anything!"

"Your aunt Rosa is inside, mi Marco," his mother said, ushering him closer into a hug. "Come here. Come inside. All of you. Before anyone sees."

"Aunt Rosa?" Marco took another look at the house again, his thoughts now traveling to a different time. The faded, decorative marble gnomes caught his attention again- a male and a female one in an embrace. *Si, no estoy loco!* He hadn't imagined it at all- he really *had* been at this house before. A long time ago, as a little boy, holding his mama's hand.

"*Si, mi hijo,*" Isabella answered her son, caressing his cheek while glancing between him and Pedro.

She turned to meet eyes with Delilah, who returned her smile. "I see it too, yeah. There is a little resemblance, isn't there? Wow! Oh, man! I had no idea our driver Marco could be...*the* Marco..."

"I knew it!" Pedro exclaimed, releasing laughter as they all had entered inside. The laughter sounded to Marco like it'd long been held back. "I knew he looked familiar when I saw him in the car, mom! I recognized him from his picture!"

"Si, *mi amor*," Isabella chuckled. "You and your mom had a blessing today from the hand of God- meeting my Marco. Take a seat. Aunt Rosa will be out of the shower any minute now- you poor things can wash up after she's out. In the meantime, you can wash your faces in the small bathroom we've got here downstairs...Oh, what has that *monstruo* done again..."

"*Mami*, I don't remember an Aunt Rosa?" Marco whispered, watching Delilah and Pedro be ushered toward the guest bathroom around the corner. He crossed his arms across his chest, watching as his mother returned to join him on the living room couch. Marco managed to take a look around; modern art and furniture decorated a theme of black/white/red around the space. This 'Aunt Rosa' had pretty good taste.

"Could you please finally tell me why you're here? Why any of us are here? How do you know Delilah and Pedro? And you called her husband 'monster'- do you know him or something? What in Heaven's name is going on?"

Isabella caressed his arm, her expression turning serious for the first time that evening since Marco had spotted her.

"Rosa is my cousin, *mi hijo*," she started with a sigh. "Not really your aunt, as you already know my sisters back in Colombia. We haven't kept in touch much, but you did meet her once as a young boy. She's done good for herself here, and I knew Delilah and Pedro could count on her assistance with your monster of a father. Just as you and I once had, when we arrived here. Desperate. With no one else to really turn to in New York…"

"My…father?" Marco inquired.

"Well, yes, Marco," Isabella patted his arm playfully. "Don't you remember what he'd do to me? Surely you were old enough…"

"I meant, mom- what does my father have to do with Delilah and Pedro? Didn't he get deported back home?"

"That's what I told you, to keep your fears at bay, *mi hijo*," Isabella explained. "But, no, unfortunately not. Though that bastard should have long been arrested and deported- at the very least- if not downright have dropped dead…he's been around. Securing little jobs here and there. Marrying Delilah- his tax accountant- after me. Rosa said I was crazy, at first, to help her. But she was no mistress. Esteban and I were long *finito* when she entered the picture."

"Delilah…married my father? And Pedro? He's…?" Marco couldn't brave the words to come out of his mouth. Not quite yet.

"…Is your half-brother," Isabella nodded, right as the twosome started walking back toward the living room.

"Hola!" Pedro waved with a sheepish smile.

Marco smiled at him, giving him a fist pump. He turned to face Delilah. "Ma'am…um…my bad. Delilah- how long has my father been hurting you? What did you do?"

"Too long!" Isabella cut in before Delilah could say anything. "That *monstruo* has been allowed to inflict his venom for too long! I'm so glad Delilah found my information and contacted me. She's going to get revenge for all of us, Marco-all of us!"

"By…murder?" Marco began to shake his head.

"Marco, I understand you," Pedro said. "I didn't want Papi to die, either. I'd rather he rot in jail!"

EARTH UP YOUR ROOTS

"Pedro, maybe you should head upstairs, and let the adults talk about this…" Delilah said.

"Mom, I want *him* to rot in jail, *not* you!" Pedro stood up and stormed toward the kitchen.

"Baby…" Delilah began, but Isabella got up to head toward the kitchen behind Pedro.

"I'll calm him down," she said calmly. "You two- talk."

To Marco's surprise, the woman who'd appeared to be tough as a rock until that point began to weep like a baby before him.

"My Pedro is right," Delilah began to shiver. "He's issued an alert against me- but the knife really got to his artery! Or at least, I thought so! I don't understand how he could have survived! They're going to come after me now. I don't want to go to jail! Esteban had already made my life worse- so I don't care about serving time- but I can't stand to do that to Pedro! Your mother and I had had the perfect plan… it was going to look like a kitchen accident. We were all going to restart our lives here. Rosa lives alone, and she was so nice to offer to help us. Just like she once helped you and your *mami*. Esteban hates her. I…"

"No one will be going to jail, Delilah," Marco gently placed his hands on her shoulders. "You hear me? No one except maybe my father, at least. If he survives. I'll give my testimony, too. I'm familiar with criminal law. I was going to be a cop; you know? But my wife said it'd be too dangerous, so I took up other jobs. But I know enough to know that self-defense is real. You've got nothing to worry about, Delilah. I got you."

"Thank you," Delilah mouthed.

- - - - - - - -

EARTH UP YOUR ROOTS

there once were two
villagers
who, upon herding
their sheep
and harvesting the
crops
would look up at the
sky every night
and dream of
traveling the world
accomplishing
'worldly feats'
viewing their simple
lots as defeats

one night
when the stars were
huddled together
seemingly in close
proximity
to both one another
as well as to the
earth,
the villagers asked:
'What must we do?
to make it out of this
scene, accomplish
something beyond the
routine?'

they'd reaped from
the earth
only what was meant
to be reaped and no
more
didn't harm it
beyond necessity
in an attempt to
accumulate, or
explore
their services, taken
for granted
provided nutrients
for so many
urbanites going
about their business
never making time
to look at their lives
among nature
in all their busyness

yet they've catalyzed the seeds
they- the villagers- as the enabling roots of the urbanites' deeds

as poets,
we love beauty
not the physical one
of a person or a
flower
as anyone would
naturally love those
things
but the lesser
appreciated-
beauty of the miracle
called life
beauty of sorrow
beauty of
frustration
beauty of pushing
our art
like a miraculous
baby after strenuous
labor

there's obvious
beauty in success
but a lesser obvious
one in failure
in the humility when
you lose
in acceptance when
you come up short
your empathy
increases with your
fellow sisters and
brothers of the
earth

beauty of aging
beauty of having
experienced life
beauty of gratitude
for even having a
hand to record your
contributions with
beauty of being
given a body to
inhabit
to experience all the
miracles on this
planet before our
transcendence into
the next realm
beauty of ignorance
before life's meaning
and plan
the beauty of surrender
we're beautiful
when we're in this
together

MAINTAIN

*to be called ungrateful
for being given everything
but the simple things you actually need...
         is the worst kind of mental torture*

SELIN SENOL-AKIN

we tend to reflect back on our teenage fights
with ridicule

backstabbed lives…
lover stolen
words like knives…
hearts left broken

        yet at least they'd made sense
     now you can become devalued
               for no apparent reason
grown teens trading gold for mere cents
    unanswered texts feeling like treason

yearning for the grievances
of the teenage years:

more logic behind the shed tears
less of the silent, intimidated fears

EARTH UP YOUR ROOTS

beauty can blossom
as fast as seasonably wither
a tree can sprout and scatter greens
just as rapidly as it can become jaundiced
and diminish into smithereens

empty twigs like arms can embrace with florals
suddenly blocking your cross-street view…
"Had those fences been there, and of that hue?"

duality exists…not only in quality
dark…light….'I won't'… 'I might'
but rather a process: set, until you intervene
creating your destiny

the rose in bloom only *whispers* for attention
as does the wind, splendid in its zephyr,
into your ear
things, in May, you may or may not want to hear

the grass awaits for you to lay
for a terrestrially-cooled nap
making a king-sized bed feel like hay

oh, to be in the moment…
have we ever seen such a magnificent film,
playing before our eyes daily…?
if we can drop self-imposed duties
and heed to nature embracing us gently…

SELIN SENOL-AKIN

ORDINARY

IT WAS AN ORDINARY DAY LIKE ANY OTHER during a New York October: unseasonably cold with the winds, and unseasonably warm under the sun. The heavy rains of autumn had not yet begun, and Janice for one was feeling glad that Monday morning.

"I hope he notices my blown-out hair before any winds ruin it," she thought, observing her straightened, chocolate-brown long hair in her locker mirror. It had merely been a week since she had turned 14 years old, yet Janice had been feeling like she was much older for about a decade now.

Ever since her father had left her and her mother to fend for themselves in a run-down, one-bedroom apartment in Queens when she had just been a preschooler, she'd had to overhear more adult conversations than she could fully understand. For the past year or so, however-things had taken a turn for the worse, ever since her mother found out that he'd remarried a woman with a son from another man.

Suzan, her panicky mother, would constantly be on the phone with either her sister- Aunt Louise- or her lawyer friend, Jack. "Find out how much he is spending on that woman and her boy, now," Suzan would suggest, often mistaking Jack for a private detective. "He'd better not be neglecting both his child support *and* spousal support in order to accommodate for someone else's bastard child! And find out if his company really *is* in trouble this quarter as he claims…"

Janice never understood why Jack would allow himself to be subjected to such extra labor, and for such a small legal fee at that. As everyone knew- lawyers were supposed to be money-hungry folks, weren't they? *He must have had a crush on my poor mother ever since they used to work together*, she'd secretly suspected. *Why else?*

Men were interested in only one thing, her mother would continuously warn her- especially as she had just entered high school that previous month. *Whatever,* Janice thought, her heart beating faster the minute she heard Scott's infectious laughter as he rounded the corner. He was joking about something with one of his football teammates. She shut her locker door and cleared her throat as Scott approached. "Hey Janice, how's it going?"

"Hey Scott, can't complain actually..." Janice stammered, flipping her hair over her left shoulder. "And you? This weather has been so weird, hasn't it?"

"Hey, yeah, I've got to go...Sorry...I'll see you tomorrow in Chem," Scott said as he hurried down the corridor to catch up with his friend.

His friend, Janice thought to herself, with an exasperated sigh. *That's all I'll probably ever be as well. His Chemistry partner in class...while he remains the quarterback of my dreams.*

§

"Mom, this is absolutely delicious," Janice exclaimed over dinner later that evening. "This is a different sauce you've used on these chicken cutlets. Do I taste oregano? Basil?"

"It's just a bunch of spices thrown together over some extra olive oil drizzle, honey," Suzan stated with an expressionless face. She'd already cleaned off her plate and was just accompanying her daughter at the table as she ate. "I just wanted to liven it, up. I'm glad you like it."

EARTH UP YOUR ROOTS

"...Okay. Mom? Mom!" Janice didn't like the subtle sadness she heard in her mother's voice. "Are you okay?"

"Oh, I'm fine," Suzan started, grabbing a slice of toasted bread from the basket in the middle of the table. "It's nothing...just that Jack was supposed to stop by for dinner tonight, too, and, well, I haven't heard from him yet..."

"Oh, I see" Janice started to feel her blood begin to boil. "So, this atypical, non-bland chicken was for Jack, apparently, and not me. Cool."

"Don't start, Janice," Suzan warned, nibbling nervously on her slice. "You know he's got his report on your father ready and was just supposed to come over to discuss it, but..."

"Speaking of the devil..." Janice mocked, peering at her mother's cell phone after a text message made a sound.

"Yes- your father definitely *is that* for putting us through this..." Suzan started, picking up her phone with excitement.

"I meant Jack, mom" Janice said, rolling her eyes. "Mr. Lawyer-of-the-year has some excuse for being late, apparently."

"Stuck in traffic...I'm on my way. My apologies..." Suzan read with a smile.

"Joy," Janice said. "I'll be in my room

while you two discuss how *devilish* my father apparently is."

"Don't you take that tone with me, young lady," Suzan started. "Do you really want to see your mother continue to struggle while your father is frolicking with some woman, and…?"

"They're *married*, mom!" Janice exclaimed. "And, yes, of course I'm not exactly thrilled he left us…and I appreciate your two part-time jobs, trying to make ends meet. I mean, hey, I'm going to start babysitting soon. But dad does *still* care. I mean he got me my laptop for my birthday…"

"Clever, honey," Suzan started, standing up to pace back and forth around the kitchen. "That's what that man is. For *buying* your acceptance and affections!"

"Looks like our savior is here," Janice mocked as she heard the 'ding dong' of the doorbell.

"Shh, not another negative word from you," Suzan warned with a whisper. "Please. We need him to extract extra financial support from your father, you know this…"

Janice pretended to zip her lips, rolling her eyes once again toward the ceiling.

§

"Mr. Stevens…you really didn't have to…" Janice started to say later over coffee in the living room.

"*Jack*. I insist, Janice, please call me by my first name," the lawyer said with a smile, as he fixed his designer-brand glasses on his angular face.

"Ok…Jack," Janice continued. "I mean, I've forgotten about my birthday already….And, this smart phone…It's the latest model! It's really too much, I can't accept this…"

"You've raised a really humble teenager, right here, Suzan," Jack smiled, turning next to him to face Suzan- who was grinning from ear to ear.

"She's one of a kind, my Janice. But, she's right. This is awfully too sweet of you…You've already been so kind, and…"

"Nonsense," Jack insisted. "Ladies, ladies…believe me…you both deserve nothing but the best. After everything you've had to go through as mother and daughter…"

"Would you like another cup?" Suzan asked, pointing at the coffee machine.

"No, thank you," Jack interrupted this time. "Please, just, sit down…"

Suzan did as she'd been told, exchanging an equally nervous and silent look with her daughter.

"To start off with the good news," Jack began, taking out a printed photograph from the backpack which he had placed next to his feet, "Here, you can see Bob and Laura leaving an IKEA, holding hands…"

"Just wonderful," Suzan mocked.

"*IKEA*, Suzan," Jack retorted, pulling out another computer-scan of a different, close-up photo now. "Not buying some fancy, expensive furniture like you had been imagining. And- if you look closely at Laura's ring finger here in this photo- you can tell that she's wearing a simple wedding band, nothing too..."

"Ok, ok, I get it, Jack, thank you…." Suzan was shaking her head and covering her eyes with her left palm now. "I know you must mean well- but honestly seeing them isn't helping…"

"Suzan, look," Jack started with a sigh. "You asked me to ensure he wasn't spending more money on them while refusing to increase his child and spousal support for you and Janice. Not, may I remind you, to appease your apparent jealousy over their relationship!"

"You… You've misunderstood," Suzan exclaimed, clearing her throat. "Of course, I'm grateful for the truth. And I could care less about what Bob feels anymore…It's just…"

"…What I believe my mom is trying to say, Jack, is *thank you*," Janice cut in, sarcasm audible in her monotone voice. "I've been telling her- it's all in her head…"

"Janice, that's enough…" Suzan started with an angry tone.

"Let her speak, Suzan," Jack stated. "She's not a child anymore- listen to your daughter…Go ahead, Janice."

"Um, thank you," Janice continued. "I mean, I actually met up with my dad for my birthday recently, and we had a long and honest discussion. He is working extra hard to provide for everyone. He seemed happier than I'd ever seen him…"

"Thank *you*, Janice," Suzan said in a softer, exasperated voice. "You've embarrassed me in front of Jack. And thanks for sympathizing with your father's *holy* search for happiness, while I'm…"

"Mom, please stop needlessly victimizing yourself," Janice stood up to sit next to her mother on the opposite end of the couch, placing her hand on her shoulder. "I love you…and I want nothing but for you to move on with your life and find happiness, as well…"

"I'm…embarrassed…," Suzan said with

a smile now. "Ok, Jack, please tell us the bad news, I suppose, before we take any more of your time tonight."

"No worries," Jack said with a smile. "Well, the only bad news, I suppose, is- yes, like Janice has learned...I found out further details about his extra hours, actually. Bob has been doing some extra research apparently on the computer- the details of which I couldn't get yet. But- here's the catch- he's definitely working on it with Laura. I've seen them going over details at various coffee shops. They may have been able to land some well-paying side project, for all we know..."

"This is it?" Janice mocked, after observing her mom's silent, acceptant nodding. "Mom- this is pure speculation and guessing..."

"I really don't know what to say..." Suzan started, putting both of her hands in the air.

"...Mom," Janice cut in, taking a peek at a text message that had just arrived on her old cell phone. "Clara is asking for help with our Social Studies homework. Can I stop by her place for half an hour?" Clara was her best friend who lived just two buildings down her block.

"Well, you know the rules," Suzan started. "As long as you make it back before 11..."

"I've got to get going too, actually," Jack said as he got up. "I'll walk the young lady out. If you guys need, I can even catch up on some e-mails in my car and wait for her return, to walk her back. You can never know what kind of shady people could be looming out there during these late hours…"

"Oh, thank you, Jack," Janice started, grabbing her backpack from her room, where she'd gone to fetch her textbook. "But, I go there all the time, I mean‚‚‚"

"We'd love that, Jack," Suzan cut in. "Very kind of you to offer, actually- thank you. I would feel a lot more at ease…"

"Alright…I guess. After you…." Janice said, putting on her jacket as she shot her mother an annoyed look over her shoulder. "I'll see you soon, mom."

"Good night, Suzan," Jack called out from the elevator doors as they opened. "Everything will be alright."

§

As Janice started to hurry back home forty minutes later, she cursed her luck when she noticed just then that soft rain had started. "Oh, shoot!" she exclaimed, trying to make sure the hood of her coat was enough to cover most of her hair as she walked to her apartment building. *So much for the sleeker style I was hoping Scott would perhaps notice better tomorrow in class*, she thought.

"Janice.... how was your study date?" Jack's voice called just then, rolling down the window of the passenger side of his new-looking Toyota sports car, sparkling with the rain drops.

Oh, darn! I'd forgotten all about him, Janice thought as she rolled her eyes. *Why couldn't he have just gone home already?* "It was good, thanks for waiting," she muttered. "I've got to go inside. This rain…"

"Of course," Jack called out. "Could you come inside for a second, though? I wanted to discuss something I couldn't do so in front of your mother, actually…"

Oh brother, thought Janice. "Well…. can it wait? It's almost 11…and you know my mom…"

"It's important…," Jack insisted.

Maybe he's learned something important about my father, Janice thought as she nodded and opened the door to take a seat on the passenger seat- which had been warmed up, to her surprise.

"How does that feel…do you like that?" Jack asked her with a smile, looking at the seat.

"Um…yeah, I guess," Janice stammered. "So, what is it that you wanted to tell me?"

"Janice…Janice…Janice," Jack started, picking on a strand of her hair from her face, as he slowly lowered the hood of her jacket back over her shoulders. "You have so much pressure on your shoulders, with all the additional stress your mother's causing with her excessive worrying. You know, I've known you for years now…I practically watched you grow up. I really admire this strong, amazing, *beautiful* young woman you've become…"

"Mr. Stevens…thank you," Janice started, a sudden chill of nerves running throughout her body, as she tried with her right hand to locate the handle of the car to run out. "But if you're not going to tell me something about the research case, then I really have to go…"

"You have no reason to feel nervous, Janice," Jack said with a smile as he started to massage her shoulders. "I just wanted to make sure a young lady like you feels relaxed and strong in times of stress like this. I can help you. I'm your friend, you know. You can call me anytime. Why haven't you started to use your new phone already? You deserve nothing but the best…"

"I don't need a massage, Mr. Stevens," Janice insisted, raising her voice now. "…Or a new telephone. I can return it to you, if you'd like. Now, excuse me, I'm going back home."

"…Alright," Jack said with a serious face now, retreating back to his seat. "You think about it, alright? I don't need the phone back. I really want you to have it…I could just use friendly conversation. Your mom can be a little too much sometimes, as you know…"

"Please don't talk about my mother like that. She actually values you and your friendship. Goodnight…" Janice stated angrily as she shut the door behind her and ran inside her apartment, not daring to look back. Her hair was getting really wet now, but she no longer cared. She didn't want to touch the hood of her jacket to cover her hair- not since it was something he had touched.

§

"Janice…Janice!" Suzan shouted the next morning, placing the porcelain plate of cheese toast and blueberries loudly in front of her daughter. "Can you please tell me what *exactly* has been bothering you ever since you returned home last night?"

"Mom, I told you," Janice said with a soft, defenseless voice. "Clara just said something that had me a little upset, but I'll get over it. It's no big deal. Chill. Would you let it go already?"

"I will not let it go!" Suzan exclaimed, taking a seat across from Janice at the table now, sipping from her warm tea mug. "You always share with me everything that bothers you about your friends. Why can't you share with me today? Is it something about a boy?"

"Oh, it's about a…guy…alright," Janice said with a mocking chuckle, still staring at her toast.

"Could you please start eating, honey?" Suzan asked in a softer, satisfied tone now. "And let me know who this mysterious guy is that you apparently had a fight about with Clara?"

"Mom, I didn't have a fight with Clara over some boy, alright?" Janice exclaimed, taking a bite of her toast and chewing on it for longer than necessary. "Just please don't push it today…"

"But you *did* just say it was about a boy…," Suzan insisted. "What else could it be? I hope you didn't give a similar attitude to Jack after you left your friend's house all angry like this…"

"Jack?" Janice retorted, standing up from her chair. "*F*** Jack!* I'm going to school, mom!"

"You watch your mouth, young lady," Suzan stood up after her. "I told you there will be no cursing in this house! What is *with* your hostility towards Jack? He's been nothing but good…"

"Oh, he's trying to be *good* alright, mom" Janice started to say right in front of the door with her backpack over her shoulders now. "He's trying to be *really good*- especially to me- to *me*- mom. I'm freaking 14 years old! Don't you see? The guy is a creep! Okay? Are you satisfied?"

"Whoa, there..." Suzan said, as she blocked the door so that her daughter couldn't leave just yet. "What exactly are you trying to imply here, Janice? That because he bought you a birthday gift…and, wanted to wait for you to make sure you got back home safe…?"

"Mom, no!" Janice started, throwing her backpack on the floor. "The phone is still in its box in my drawer- you can go ahead and use it if you'd like. I don't want it! I don't want anything that man touched- not after he touched my hair and my face in his car, and my shoulders..."

"Janice?" Suzan yelled. "Did he downright do something inappropriate...?"

"Mom!" Janice exclaimed in shock. "I'm telling you the man touched my face...and he massaged my shoulders. How much more *inappropriate* does he have to get...?"

"Jack has always been just a friendly guy," Suzan said, holding her daughter's shoulders now. "Now, listen to me: you will not breathe a word about your silly suspicions to anyone, alright?"

"Mom, he admitted he watched me grow up," Janice said as she started to tear up. "He was never particularly friendly with me when I was younger! Why won't you believe me?"

"I'm not saying that," Suzan said. "I'm just afraid you may be exaggerating...That's all."

"I'm going to school now," Janice said with a loud sigh, wiping her tears on the sleeve of her coat. "All I know is, I don't ever want to be alone with that man, ever again. Alright? Please..."

§

"Are you OK?" Scott asked, sorting out three different test tubes at the laboratory table.

"You've been pretty distracted today…I mean, you're also *pretty*, as always, but distracted." He added a smile.

"That's sweet, Scott" Janice said, returning his smile. She couldn't believe her luck. Scott was finally paying closer attention her- it seemed- and despite her frizzed-up hair, at that. Yet, she couldn't help but continue to be traumatized over not only having been hit on by her mother's long-term friend in his car, but also by her mother's apparent denial. "I just had a minor spat with my mom, that's all."

"Ouch!" Scott said. "I have those all the time too, believe me. My mom and I have been increasingly more and more awkward with each other, especially since we just moved in with her new husband in Brooklyn. Which reminds me, I may have to switch to a new school closer to the new place, soon."

"Brooklyn? Are you serious?" Janice's day was looking like it'd be becoming increasingly sadder.

"Kids! Back to work! No chatting!" Mr. Brown called out from the front of the class.

"Sorry!" Janice and Scott called out to their Chemistry teacher, giggling.

"But, Janice, you've got to check out my new room, though," Scott said in a lowered voice, showing pictures from his cell phone to Janice now from under the lab table. "It's so cool- the way Bob and my mom decorated it- and much bigger than my room here in Queens."

Bob! Janice felt a chill run up her spine the minute her father's name had been uttered by Scott.

"Scott?" she asked. "Do you happen to have a picture of your new stepfather as well?"

"My stepfather?" Scott asked with a confused face, reaching for his cell. "Oh, you mean Bob? He's cool, I guess. Hold on, let me see. Here you go! They're like teenagers. It's so awkward…"

As Scott showed her a photograph of himself as the witness for his mother and her father at their court wedding ceremony, Janice got a sinking feeling in the pit of her stomach.

"I'm afraid it's about to get more awkward, Scott," she stated softly. "Let's wrap this up before Mr. Brown sends us to Detention, and talk after class…"

§

"Wow!" Scott exclaimed later that afternoon, sipping on his Java-Chip cold drink at the Starbucks two blocks from their school.

"We...are officially...step-siblings: my good old Chem partner and I, huh? Oh, man!"

"...Yup...," Janice replied with a nervous chuckle. She couldn't even bring herself to order anything to drink. She was feeling shocked at both the surprising news, as well as the speed at which her little crush had begun to feel more platonic the moment she realized the truth.

"I mean, he told us he had a daughter," Scott continued. "But he never gave any details. It doesn't really surprise me, though. He and mom are always busy working on secretive stuff together...If I didn't know any better, I'd fantasize they were CIA agents or something," Scott chuckled.

"Secretive...stuff?" Janice asked, recalling the curious project Jack had told them he'd seen Laura and her father working on, thinking it could potentially have been some side hustle.

"Well...it's actually not so secretive, I guess," Scott explained, putting his drink down and letting out a big sigh. "It's actually kind of gross, but necessary...Are you ready to hear this?"

"Gross...but necessary?" Janice asked with a raised eyebrow. "Curiosity killed the cat. Tell me!"

EARTH UP YOUR ROOTS

"Well, my mom is an attorney, you see…" Scott began. "She's particularly passionate about putting pedophiles behind bars- that sort of thing. And Bob- your dad- is good with computers, as you know. So, I know they most recently received some tips about some pervert that's been showing his face in Queens. Apparently, the guy served a little time for child pornography distributions and gross things like that, and had practically been shunned from Elmhurst, Woodside, Corona and the entire area here basically! But one of the victim's mothers swore she started seeing him drive around the neighborhood in some fancy car- in disguise apparently with glasses…"

Just as Janice started getting goosebumps at the memory of Jack touching her in his car the previous night, she also couldn't ignore the need she felt for her next question. "Scott…does this guy have a name?"

"Well, I'm supposed to keep quiet until they've collected more evidence …" Scott continued sheepishly. "I mean- you know, with the whole *innocent until proven guilty* thing…"

"Scott, please," Janice pleaded. "There's this creepy friend my mother brings over to the house sometimes, but he sort of hit on me and he wears glasses and drives a fancy car, like you said...."

"Whoa," Scott exclaimed. "Janice, that's some serious stuff...Did you tell your mom?"

"I did..." Janice began, tears welling up in her eyes. "But she's sort of in denial...Scott, please! Tell me the name!"

"Jack. The creep's name is Jack Stevens. Does it ring a bell?"

§

The subway ride to Brooklyn (after Janice had to plead with her mother to allow her to go see her father for 'bonding time' after her 'car trauma') was mostly quiet in awkward silence.

"Would you like some lemonade while we wait for Bob, honey?" Laura asked once they'd reached the humble two-bedroom place where she lived with Scott and Janice's father.

"No, thanks," Janice said with a smile. "And thank you again for agreeing to see me and listen to everything, on such short notice..."

"Oh Janice, of course," Laura started, smiling at her son who'd been eating his sandwich next to Janice at the kitchen table. "Scott's always talked about you as one of his favorite friends at school. And I recognized your name from the teenage daughter Bob always talks so fondly of-but I never thought it would actually be *you*...you know? Life works in mysterious ways..."

"I agree," Janice said, looking the plump woman up and down. She seemed like a humble lady- the complete opposite of her mother's thin frame always adorned with extra accessories. Each time Laura mentioned her father's name, Janice could hear the sound of affection in her voice.

Janice sighed as she recalled her mother's warning on the phone as she very reluctantly agreed to allow her to go to her father's house. *Don't you dare complain about Jack when he hasn't done anything bad to you. We still need him. Please Janice...Be smart.*

"...This is him, yes...?" Laura asked after she'd opened some files on her laptop. "This is the bastard. Jack Stevens."

As Janice took a deep breath and braced herself with what she was about to see, she was pleasantly surprised when Scott gave her arm a reassuring pat. She smiled, as she felt just then that it had truly felt brotherly. As an only child, she'd often wondered about what it would have been like to have a sibling. *Who knew?* She thought. *I guess something was bound to connect me to him after all.*

Looking at the familiar face on the screen- a current photo of Jack with glasses, as well as an older photograph of him posing without glasses with some former students- Janice sat down on a nearby couch in their living room and covered her eyes with her hands.

"Hey, hey, it's alright," Laura said as she came to sit down next to her. "If it's him- you'd be helping us catch a predator we'd been looking for, for so long. Mrs. Nunez for one would be very happy to meet you- a catalyst in the capturing of the pervert that traumatized her daughter. That little girl still has nightmares, apparently…"

This is it, Janice thought. *This is where I can lie and say I don't recognize him, or tell the truth, and make a difference in people's lives: perhaps even in my own and that of my mother's.*

"Stop needlessly victimizing, yourself Janice," Suzan had told her on the phone before she'd gotten on the train. "That's what you told me too last night- remember?"

Her mother's voice had sounded more vengeful- for somehow embarrassing her in front of Jack- rather than concerned.

I'm not victimizing myself, mom, Janice thought just then. *Just the opposite, in fact.*

"That's him," Janice said confidently.

EARTH UP YOUR ROOTS

As the doorbell rang and Scott allowed Bob to enter, Janice looked at her father with a smile. "Dad…" she called out.

"Oh, honey…honey…Laura filled me in a bit. Never doubt your instincts, sweety," Bob said as he walked over to hug his daughter. "I wish I could have warned you guys sooner…I wish you'd told me right away."

§

The events of that following week after the revelation were still fresh in Janice's mind, even now that almost exactly an entire year had gone by. Janice, a sophomore in high school, with her stepbrother Scott now attending school in Brooklyn- where they'd continued to hang out from time to time whenever she'd spend time with her father- was eating spiced-chicken with her mom for dinner again. "I hope this delicious chicken isn't for another man again, mom," Janice said with a playful wink that particularly cold October evening.

"Oh, hush," Suzan replied with a smile. "It was never about a man…Especially not that a-hole, whose name will never be uttered in this house again- may he rot behind bars. You know,

I just wanted to believe I could somehow marry again and provide a family for you again…Like your father did so easily, you know…"

"Mom," Janice said, taking her mother's hand in hers. "We *are* a family."

"When did you grow up?" Suzan asked with a tear forming in her right eye as she squeezed back her daughter's hand. "I'm so proud of you. *Nana* would have been proud, too."

"Sometimes adults are the children, and the children have to be the adults…" Janice retorted with a laugh.

"Yeah, yeah" Suzan laughed. "You and your sayings. My daughter's going to be a writer…a famous writer. She's no ordinary girl, I know it. You know: my friend Tim is actually a published author…I'm telling you; you have to send him some of your work sometime…"

Janice didn't reply. She just smiled and allowed her mom to continue talking, and later changed the subject.

EARTH UP YOUR ROOTS

the glistening raindrop
clings to the grass
capturing attention
which the mind can
but the spirit will *not* deny

this drop will soon perish
in the heat of the sun
when the clouds part
while its fleeting memory
will remain in the flooded heart

the rooted grass, of course, will stay
going about its day-to-day
even when the snow will come, cover,
and eventually melt away

moments gone by
will always be the most admired
nostalgically desired
until we die

SELIN SENOL-AKIN

the familiar sounds of the morning
the hammers doing fixing
the birds doing chirping
the employees commuting

the familiar view
or the familiar smell, a nasal hue
the stench of brewed tea or coffee,
the moist soil lingering from rain, lovely dew

mentally organizing your daily tasks
not realizing it may be your last
death could come indeed
at any moment
pray, take heed

death of the body…death of employment
death of love…death of enjoyment

you're prepared for anything on this earth
as long as your mind is prepared for its rebirth

BLOOM

*those who overestimate themselves
will underestimate you,
likely never having been told
the story of the tortoise and the hare as a child*

SELIN SENOL-AKIN

the rain nourishes the hopping, content sparrow
fulfilling its most natural need
through this occurrence, unpredictable
but nonetheless reliable

the rain
which brings harmony into the soul
accumulating subtly at first…drop by drop
until the sudden outpour…floods now with joy
unpredictable…undeniable

it washes away settled dust on cars
and creaky fences
the rain creates chances
to glow
where you can tolerate the chill
or give into the thrill
of a subsequent *rainbow*

EARTH UP YOUR ROOTS

I got a bruise yesterday
not sure how
but it spread, dark and throbbing
...sure as I know where my head I lay

some bruises have a mysterious root
better those
than wounds remnant from youth

I wear the scars, invisible, though tattooed
I smile away the chagrin;
when there's a will, there's a way

I apologize
for all the times

I didn't listen
to the little girl
begging for my attention

both to my daughter
and to my reflection
in the mirror

life repeats
until your lesson
becomes clearer

SELIN SENOL-AKIN

ZELLE

A PLAY

Prologue

1889. Leeuwarden, Netherlands. Dutch music is playing. A teenage girl with long wavy brown hair is dancing alone in front of a sunny window overlooking a meadow.

Adam Zelle: M'greet! M'greet! Come down for dinner, please! Your brothers are already at the table. Your ill mother has managed to still prepare a lovely dinner for us all- do not anger her!

Margaretha: I'm coming, father. *(Smiles proudly at her silhouette's reflection on the window. Turns to her mirror in movement. Whispers under her breath)*

As if you haven't angered her enough.

(Humming a melody, holds up her skirt and twirls)

I cannot be to blame.... I am merely dreaming....

EARTH UP YOUR ROOTS

ACT 1.

Living Room. 1897. Java, Dutch East Indies (Indonesia). RUDOLF and MARGARETHA are in conversation.

Rudolf: (*clears his throat*) Margaretha?

Margaretha continues folding some napkins distractedly. Her focus is outside the window.

Rudolf: (*adds louder*) Margaretha Zelle!

Margaretha: Hmm? Oh, sorry. I was lost in thought about something Lady Bella said over dinner. What is it?

Rudolf: You were distracted when our guests were here, too. Yes. Don't think your husband hasn't noticed. I can tell when you're daydreaming again, even by a flutter of those eyelashes.

Margaretha: *(puts the napkins, in a pile, back in a cupboard)* No, not at all, Rudolf. You've got it wrong, this time. I was merely still thinking about what she'd mentioned about those dances for the gods. I wonder what they look like. Otherwise- no dreams of working again. Do not worry. I've promised you.

Rudolf: *(satisfied, picks up his newspaper again and plays with his mustache)* Good girl. If you remain honest like this with me, then I should count my blessings once again that you've answered my ad for a spouse, and not some other gal.

Margaretha: *(rolls her eyes and forces a smile)* You can rest assured, Rudolf. I'm well aware of my duties to you and this household, in return for this fortunate life here with you. I have, after all, been reminded countless times. You can concentrate on the news once again.

Rudolf: Oomph, the news isn't very pleasant, I'm afraid. Drums of violence and aggression are sounding from the West. As a man of the military- I must be confident that I have a loving wife at home, focused on growing our family and performing her tasks. So that I may have my load lightened and be able to focus on my mission.

EARTH UP YOUR ROOTS

Margaretha: *(under her breath)* Yes, that's also the job description of a servant, isn't it?

Rudolf: *What* did you say?

Margaretha: Nothing. Simply that I understand.

Rudolph: *(grabs her arm)* I heard you, Margaretha Zelle. You mentioned that word again. 'Servant'.

Margaretha: It was merely a joke. Let go of my arm, please. You're hurting it again.

Rudolf: *(relentless):* You are never to equate being a dutiful wife with servitude again, Margaretha Zelle. Do you understand me? Servitude is being loyal to one's nation. I hope to be clearer this time.

Margaretha: *(whispers, her eyes looking at the head of the house maids in the other room)* Maria will hear. You are clear. Now, let go. I apologize.

Rudolf: *(softens his grip, transforming it into a graze on her cheek)* Good girl. That's the one I married. This side of you. The side of you who is aware that some sacrifices are made in a marriage by both sides. I always return to you my side of the marriage contract too, do I not?

Margaretha: *(changes her voice tone into a playful one)* Oh, do you? But you've been too distracted lately, Rudolf MacLeod. For 2 months to be exact. Yes, I've been counting. You haven't even really touched me since you began that new…

Rudolf: *(pulls her torso closer to his and whispers into her ear)* I will make it up to you, my Zelle. I told you. I'm an older man- I need my rest. The long hours have been taking a toll.

(kisses her softly on the lips). Let's sleep tonight, and you'll be a happy girl over this coming weekend. In the meantime, did you try on the new bracelet?

Margaretha: The golden one? Oh, yes, it was very exotic. Thank you. I adored it.

Rudolf: It's a specialty of the Indies.

Margaretha: (*sighs and locks eyes with MARIA, who's closer to them now, fluffing some pillows*)

Yes. You've got quite a taste for this island's specialties, indeed.

Maria: I'm done for the evening, sir. Madam. May I be excused?

Rudolf: (*smiles*): You may go, Maria. Thank you.

Maria: (*smiles back with a bow, meeting his gaze for a long moment with blushing cheeks*) Goodnight.

ACT II

Scene 1

Paris, France. 1905. Fancy restaurant. Music playing. LOUISE and MARGARETHA are dining.

Louise: You have got to show me those moves again, *chérie*. I could use one or two of them on good old Mr.Hubbert. Our anniversary is coming up. Lord knows we need a little spice (*she laughs and sips her wine*)

Margaretha: *(laughs confidently, throwing her hair back)* I could. But I'd have to charge you, *ma chérie amie*. After all, I'm a professional entertainer now, educated in this art of dance. Have you not noticed?

Louise *(laughs with her):* Oh, I've noticed. I think this entire restaurant has noticed. Simply even that hat of yours is enough!

Margaretha: Oh, Louise. Soon enough, it will not just be my clothes or my hats. Or just this restaurant. Soon enough this entire city and the entirety of France- and perhaps even Europe- will know my name. They'll know my face. My story. My dance.

Louise: *(looks around and lowers her voice to a whisper)* Of course, *chérie*. You know I'm your best supporter. But surely you know, you've got to be careful. They're talking about you, too. You know. How you've left your surviving child with your ex-husband, and come here for your- and I quote- 'selfish, promiscuous striptease'.

Margaretha: *(bursts into tears)* I'm working on it, Louise. And of course I am aware of the pitiable slander.

Louise: *(gets up to sit next to her and caresses her arms)* I'm sorry. I just wanted to ensure your preparation before any potential conflict these jealous folks may concoct.

Margaretha: *(wipes away a tear and waves her fingers dismissively)* It's not just their hurtful words, my dear friend. Even your name-Louise. I'm constantly reminded…*Ma fille*… My Louise Jeanne. I miss her so terribly. I couldn't afford to keep her; despite being given custody. But it's even more than that. After losing our dear, little

Norman to that sickness... I couldn't bear not giving Louise a better life! And I knew...she'd be better off without me. Prouder, perhaps- hopefully- of a happier mommy, making a name for herself across Europe. Rather than a sad one back in Java- or even in the Netherlands now - living with that monster.

Louise: You're sure Rudolf can be trusted as a father, right?

Margaretha: Oh, yes. Of that, I'm certain. I'll admit he was a formidable father- if not a great husband. As for me- I'm afraid I couldn't be either- neither an ideal wife nor a mother. Perhaps that's why I'm trying so hard to be a good dancer, Louise. To be good at *something*. Once I'm ready- I know she will come live with her mommy. I just know it. I will earn her heart. I will deserve it.

Louise: *(rubs her back)* Of course, *bien sur*.

Margaretha: *(clears her throat, adds a sudden smile and a wink)* Now, where were we? Oh, yes! My performances. And yours in your marital bed next week. I'll show you everything I've studied.

EARTH UP YOUR ROOTS

The moves of the Orient, India and the Sumay combined! I tell you: they're not only an aphrodisiac on the eyes, but also on the soul. That's one of my plans, dear Louise. You see?

She inches closer to her friend, clutching her wine glass tighter in her hand

They cannot continue to spread *femme fatale* rumors about me, if they know the pure and spiritual stories behind the dances! I am not merely some stripper- Lord knows there are thousands of French models here with more enticing curves than mine. It's the *story*, Louise, that these viewers also love. Beyond just the striptease. The purity…the innocence they enjoy seeing on the woman's face at the end of her seduction. It's poetry.

Louise: *(nods)* The poetry…The purity…Got it, M'greet.

Mata Hari: *(waves a finger seductively)* Non, non. *Mata Hari*. N'oubliez pas! No more *Marghereta* or *Zelle* or *M'greet*. I am ready to embody my stage name wholly now. It shall bring me luck. I will speak it- and dance it- into existence!

Louise: *(chuckles)* No resistance! Cheers to Mata Hari. What was it? Oh yes! L'oeil du soleil. Eye of the sun! Mata Hari!

Mata Hari: Cheers!

She locks eyes with all the men in the restaurant sneaking looks in the direction of the loudness from their table. Instrumental Eastern music plays in the background.

Scene 2

Streets of Paris. GABRIEL and MATA HARI are having a casual stroll.

Gabriel: May I have a word, Mata?

Mata Hari: Of course! What is it, dear Gabriel?

Gabriel: Mata, you have not only been a great client of mine to book over the past year, but also a great friend. There for me with the anti-Semitic battles I've had to battle…

Mata Hari: Oh, of course. Argh! It has surely been the most absurd thing to me- to not be accepted as a human being simply for being who you are. Go on…

Gabriel: It gives me great pleasure to announce to you the good news…

Mata Hari: Oh, prey do tell already!

Gabriel: You, my dear, are now a regular at the Paris Olympia!

Mata Hari (jumps for joy and the two hug)

ACT III

Scene 1

EMILE ETIENNE GUIMET and MATA HARI are in a Parisian hotel room.

Emile: *(looks at the B&W photograph in his hand)* A Hindu priestess, huh?

Mata Hari: *(hugs him from behind)* Oh, hush, Emile. The crowd at your precious museum gobbled it right up! The public of Europe simply adores such exotic background stories, you know that!

Emile: *Oui, ma belle*. They adore it- but do they *buy it*? That is my concern. If you begin to lose credibility, that could become the end of our business arrangement.

Mata Hari: *(plays with his hair)* Oh, no, we wouldn't want such an ending. And especially not an ending of our *personal* arrangement as well, I hope?

EARTH UP YOUR ROOTS

Emile: *(gives her a passionate kiss)* Never. I'm just concerned and you need to work extra hard to…

Mata Hari: How's your family doing, Emile? How's your old lady?

Emile: Why remind me of that now? Are you trying to make me feel bad again, after we've just made love?

Mata Hari: Well, are you trying to make *me* feel bad for my stories…?

Emile: I'm simply expressing concern….

Mata Hari: So am I, Emile! Just a *petit* reminder that it is not only I who has to be careful of the revelation of the truth, is it…?

The two turn their backs toward each other for a moment.

Look, Emile. Do not worry. Even if they are suspicious- this is my art. People can temporarily suspend disbelief for the beauty of the art in a given moment. How else do you explain the utter insistence of the story of Santa Claus around Noel?

Emile: That's a tad bit different, my silly darling…

Mata Hari: Stories are stories, Emile. And art is art.

Emile: This is work. This is life.

Mata Hari: And just what is life, if not a temporary work of art?

Emile: (*kisses the tip of her nose*) Ok, you win.

Mata Hari: I always make sure I do.

Emile: Stubborn girl. My woman-child. I want to obtain my divorce, and marry you already.

Mata Hari: *(lets out a sigh)* Doesn't always work out so easily, Emile. Look, I'm sorry for being sensitive. But…that photograph…Please throw it out…

Emile: I need something to dream about you with when we have to be away, my darling.

Mata Hari: It's just that- I know Rudolf is always up for using anything he can against me with regards to our Louise Jeanne.

EARTH UP YOUR ROOTS

Emile: I understand. Very well.

Mata Hari: Thank you. And give me another favor, will you, Emile? Don't ever talk about leaving your family for me. I never asked for it- you know that. And I never would. Your children need their father. They don't have to pay for our sins.

Emile: Darling, there's always a price for everything worth having in life.

Mata Hari: Don't I know it…

Scene 2

Performance space surrounded by crowds. MATA HARI is dancing with five other women in black around her. Wears a metal breastplate, flowing fabric tied around her hips and little else to cover up her nearly nude body. She rattles her entire torso in a spiritual trance. At the end of the dance, she drops herself on the floor. The crowd is mesmerized, silent. She suddenly puts an arm up with flair, throwing her head back in an 'innocent' smile. The crowd goes wild with applause.

EARTH UP YOUR ROOTS

ACT IV

Scene 1

1916. MATA HARI is 40 years old and chubbier now. She hasn't danced since 1915. Meets her friend LOUISE again in a home setting.

Mata Hari: I'm afraid it may be over, *mon amie*. Ten years. I've peaked. Now, it's as if I can only hang on to the sides of a steep mountain while I continue my decline…

Louise: You are still a great dancer, Mata Hari. Youth is but an illusion. You have inspired me so much! I've left Monsieur Hubert. I've got the kids. My bakery is doing well. I am standing on my own feet. All because of you- Margaretha! You're my inspiration. My hero. You cannot give up now…Not you…

Mata Hari: That's wonderful. You've got your baking talent to hang on to. What do I have? Rudolf was right- I couldn't cook for *mierde*. But did I deserve to be mistreated?

Louise: No, of course not…

Mata Hari: Men can get away with everything. It is simply not fair, Louise. Women like you with a talent or trade can certainly get more ahead now than they could before. But, regardless, at the end of the day- we are still looked upon differently…As the lesser sex, somehow.

Louise: You *do* have your trade! Maybe…you can open a dance school for girls? Teach all you've taught yourself for years?

Mata Hari: But what is a woman without her dignity, Louise? I've been hanging on to my anger for so long…Getting revenge on all the men I've seen do me wrong. My father. Rudolf. Countless lovers involved in their ridiculous politics. By doing the same…I've been using the men back, just as they've used me! But I am not happy, Louise. I cannot go to sleep with a clear conscience like you can.

Louise: It's never too late. You were not the only free-spirit of Europe. You've had countless imitators…You're a living legend!

Mata Hari: What is the worth of having a 'legend' if one couldn't actually *live* while alive?

EARTH UP YOUR ROOTS

Louise: To inspire? Through your story?

Mata Hari (*smiles*): I've always liked that...

Louise: How's the young captain?

Mata Hari (*rolls her eyes*): Vadim? Oh, you know, just being... young. A Russian pilot providing service for the French. And me as his lover- can you imagine? Old enough to be his mother... He wouldn't be with me if he hadn't had such a reckless character to begin with...

Louise: You are not that much older than him, come on. Men take on young lovers all the time, and no one cares.

Mata Hari: I'm telling you... It's a man's world! But I *am* worried about him...It's dangerous out there.

Louise: You love him...

Mata Hari: I love the way he makes me feel...

Louise: M'greet...

Mata Hari: *(sighs, lowering her head)* Alright. I love him...I have always needed an object of affection as motivation, haven't I? I've replaced dance- which I'm no longer appreciated for- with him, I suppose.

(The two women chuckle)

EARTH UP YOUR ROOTS

Scene 2

It is summertime in France. At the military intelligence agency. MATA HARI and the director of the agency- COLONEL LOUIS- are talking.

Mata Hari: Vadim Maslov! I have to see him! His eye…I've heard what happened, and…

Colonel Louis: With your Dutch citizenship, you cannot, Madame!

Mata Hari: But it is neutral in the war- I've been able to travel freely everywhere…

Colonel Louis.: It doesn't help you on the front lines, Madame. (*Adds in a whisper*) We may be able to help you, however, if you agree to spy for France. We could use someone with your neutrality. We've heard of your closeness with the German Crown Prince Wilhelm- we are in need of intelligence on the German plans. Particularly from a certain Captain Georges Ladoux…

Mata Hari: I care not for such arrangements, nor about sides during this terrible war! Please! I simply have to see Vadim! It pains me…

Colonel Louis: You shall be able to see your Russian pilot…and be provided with one million francs. Do we have a deal, madame?

Mata Hari: (*sighs*) We have a deal.

ACT V.

Scene 1. Madrid 1916. MAJOR ARNOLD KALLE and MATA HARI are conversating in an office setting.

Major Arnold Kalle: I have read the transcript of your interrogation by Sir Basil Thomson in London. You admitted your work for France.

Mata Hari: I was…under tremendous pressure. I do not care very much for France. I am haunted by the memory of the lies and gossip- allowing me to fall down from such a high place of exaltation. I've been backstabbed, I tell you. I now only wish to help Germany.

Major Arnold Kalle: What would you want to tell the Crown Prince if we allow you to see him? You swear it is your real intention to *provide* him with information, and not *obtain* on behalf of France?

Mata Hari: I know so much about their leaders. I've been personally hurt, as well. Of course, I can provide his highness with whatever information he needs- in exchange for a fair sum, of course…and discretion.

Major Arnold Kalle: Very well, Agent H-21.

Mata Hari: Who?

Major Arnold Kalle: (*smiles*) I'm looking at her.

EARTH UP YOUR ROOTS

Scene 2:

St. Lazarre Women's Prison, 1917. Paris, France. MATA HARI is writing a letter to her daughter from her cell. She read the words out loud to herself as she writes.

Ma Cherie fille,

How I long for some miracle of clemency or justice by the forces that have placed me before my oncoming death, and for me to be able to tell you how much I love you in person in place of this letter. But, alas, life has turned your idealist mother into a realist- and I'm afraid these words will likely be the last words I shall be allotted to provide you with.

I've tried, my darling, to be a warrior…. To make you proud…But they are punishing me for something that a man in my same position and shoes would have been able to scrape through without having to pay with his life….

My Louise. I hope you go on to live a life of more honor and accomplishments as not only a woman but a human being in your life than your mother was able to....

I have only done whatever I did out of love. Love for you- knowing you'd be better under your father's traditional-minded care. Love for dance...for obtaining bliss from this life given to us by the Almighty. Love for inspiration.... Love for a man- a love that led me down dangerous roads I had no intention of ever going on...May you never love as foolishly and deeply as I have...especially someone who cannot return it...Choose a safer life...

They're accusing me of giving names.... of betraying France. They say information I provided- to whom I thought were business partners and friends- caused the death of tens of thousands of soldiers! The absurdity! How could I have done that as one woman? It was all due to their own greed and violence! I was simply trying to make a living...To utilize my neutral citizenship. I was trying to help everyone- and in turn I ended up hurting myself.

I long so much for you to be proud of me...Remember this; ultimately, it was only I who

EARTH UP YOUR ROOTS

had been betrayed...Betrayed by them all...Not even my friend Vadim agreed to testify in my defense.

Never sacrifice yourself for a man, my dearest! Never! You hear? Never sacrifice your dreams, either- as long as your feel in your heart they represent your true being and are not purposely harming anyone.

'Tis better to have lived an entire book of life in short years, than a couple of chapters into prolonged years of a dull existence.

Stay well. Stay in school. And please don't believe whatever terrible things you may hear about me. They only ever wished to see me as an extension of their own evils, and as a scapegoat- remember that. I was merely creating art, my Louise. And I merely wanted to earn enough to get in your good graces once again in my older age. Stay well...stay true to your being.

Your loving mother,

M'greet

Scene 3

MATA HARI is standing before a firing squad-*sans* a blindfold. They've begun to fire away at her. After a round or two, she blows smiling, acceptant kisses at her executors and collapses on her stomach in a similar pose as one of her most famous dances. In her last thought, she imagines she's at the end of a performance on the ground instead and raises her arm- for 'applause' in her imagination. She collapses following the death of her physical body.

EARTH UP YOUR ROOTS

write in the way
              you want to read
cook in the way
              you want to eat
love in the way
          you want to be loved-

                    stand before your fears
                    as they stand before you

SELIN SENOL-AKIN

confidence blossoms
from knowing who you are
not based on what others claim
but by heeding to your own inner star

as a child the seeds had been sprinkled
but never planted firmly
always a question remained,
you'd never been satisfied entirely

you never felt thin or curvy…
                never cool or wholesome enough
neither just the right kind of emotional…
                    nor just the right kind of tough

you grew limbs like stems
from seeds barely nurtured
dependence on another's judgments
had taken place of being watered

who you were and who you've become
can now unite with
who you realize you've always been…
                age and experience bringing comfort
                      into your unique skin
your indivi***duality***-
your inner compass pulling you to the truth
                like a magnet, toward your destiny

like a miniscule traveler into the vessels,
brain and membranes;
dive deep

all the way to the root
of the issues and pain
running through your veins

face your flaws, caress them
plant affection into those unfavored seeds-
the ones you'd hidden around the stem

acceptance breeds evolution
watch your imperfection… ***blossom***

you are more than your past
you were purposely created…. ***awesome***

SELIN SENOL-AKIN

AFTERWORD

Grow your rose….in the form of prose

Dear Reader,

What hasn't been said about a rose- mostly as a symbol for youth and fleeting beauty…of love and fleeting emotions…

Like Mata Hari- a *rose,* too, is legendary… Wasn't it Shakespeare who'd asked, "What's in a name? A rose by any other name would smell as sweet…"

Well, talking about 'roots', we *could* discuss such concepts as people changing their ethnic names to assimilate into different cultures, for instance, to argue whether that's true or not in today's world…

But what about a less-famed flower? Namely, the picture on the cover of this book- a *tulip.*

EARTH UP YOUR ROOTS

the wilting…
the pricking…
oh, I'd rather be the tulip, than the rose:
cyclical,
cultural,
perfunctory in the kitchen, in place of an onion…
growing despite being cut…
bending toward the light

Beloved reader,

If you're familiar with anything regarding Turkish culture and history, the tulip on the cover represents my roots in Türkiye; the tulip, originating in Anatolia and Central Asia rather than the Netherlands as many people think, is the country's official flower.

It is a flower that has culturally come to represent perfect love, rebirth, royalty and forgiveness…. Tulips are also known for their rather fleeting periods of bloom in the spring…Aren't we all ultimately fleeting in existence on this terrestrial realm? I often write about aging in my poems, and more from a reflective perspective rather than a mournful one; I find myself rather more

SELIN SENOL-AKIN

confident in my skin and identity at my current age, in fact, than I did in my 20's. I agree, for instance, with those who often say they wish to be able to have had their older mindset and wisdom in their younger selves and bodies.

In my previous collections, I'd written two personal poems regarding turning 35 and 36.

Well, in this one, dear reader- these 'ROOTS' are being earthed up at 37, blooming as I turn 38.

this is 37
many have delivered hell, while promising heaven

six figures desired
a dream admired
but my weary soul is getting tired

no more highs off of pointless jealousy
double standards and hypocrisy
phantoms that lead to nowhere- just let me be!

I feel more loved on my own
than by words expressed but never shown

EARTH UP YOUR ROOTS

this is 38
extinguishing flames
while circling heaven's gate

of mistakes, I'm aware
naivete gone- both the 'truth' and the 'dare'

enemies of emotions, beware

I carry still the childhood-stemmed burden
I've taught while still learning- of this, I'm certain

loving words becoming shamed
with claims of keeping sensitivities protected

endangerment of the body
and peace of mind ignored-
actions of desire instead getting respected

in this generation where benefits get exalted:
wear at least your conscience on the sleeve
even if the heart must be kept vaulted

SELIN SENOL-AKIN

just as words- we, too, are rooted

consider a Hippocratic oath
rooted as 'horse power'

versus a hypocrite
rooted as an 'actor'

distinctly reputed…

inform
set free your own form

don't conform
to the norm

make peace with ease
earth up your roots…

if you cut yourself off from them, you may become
ornamental

like roses in a vase
but with a cause and an end-
ultimately detrimental

EARTH UP YOUR ROOTS

Dear bud,

In this collection, we saw different characters affected by their 'roots' in different ways...

May you always earth up your roots and your essence, accept your unique self and your lineage with the good and the bad...

Focus on and manifest *only the good* from here out...

> FOCUS ON WHERE YOUR SOUL IS ROOTED
> NOT WHERE YOUR BODY IS LOCATED

Thank you, dear reader, for continuing this 'sowing' journey with me.

May you always ***write out your drops***, ***set free your flow***, and ***earth up your roots***.

SELIN SENOL-AKIN

right now, what's visible
may be the rotting
they can look and not see
the fruits you are slowly bearing
and the beauty you are creating
let them assume…

while you're about to bloom

EARTH UP YOUR ROOTS

the over-thinker...

SELIN SENOL-AKIN

S'ELementals
#EARTHUPYOURROOTS

ABOUT THE AUTHOR

SELIN SENOL-AKIN is a political scientist and adjunct language instructor, aside from her creative writing and featured spoken/published poetry.

The Catalyst, which reached the online new release chart at #1 during the pandemic- and won an 'Honorable Mention' award in the 2022 International Readers' Favorite Awards- is now being re-released as a trilogy: with *The Penance* (a #1 release in Scandinavian Literature in 2022*)*, and *The Nestlings* to follow, respectively.

She's also the author of two other #1 release poetic collections, *Write Out Your Drops* and *Set Free Your Flow* (half poetry/half coming-of-age memoir).

She lives in New York with her young daughter and family.

Visit selinsenolakin.com for updates

SELIN SENOL-AKIN

EARTH UP YOUR ROOTS

SELIN SENOL-AKIN

Collaborations including the author:

- 'Versos Estivales' (2019): multi-author poetry
- 'Flash' (2020)- multi-author short stories
- 'The Media High School Journal of Academics & Fiction' (2021)
- 'Write Out Your Drops'- audiobook version (2021) with Esra Gultakin as co-narrator
- 'The Catalyst'- audiobook format (2021), narrated by Katherine Schooler

www.ingramcontent.com/pod-product-compliance
Lightning Source LLC
Chambersburg PA
CBHW072015070526
44583CB00015B/1493